Trump Trial II:

Punitive Damages and Vow to Appeal

From the SDNY Trial to the 2024 Trail

By Matthew Russell Lee (c) 2024

Inner City Press

January 16 to 26, 2024

Table of Contents

I.

The night before the second Carroll - Trump trial it was colder in Iowa than in New

York. Still, the first snow in 700 days drifted down on Worth Street in front of the courthouse, where the NYPD barricades had already been set up. The circus was about to begin. And Kurt Wheelock began to get ready.

Well before the 9:30 am kickoff Trump was at the defense table, whispering with Alina Habba all dressed in white. There was a third lawyer, not in the docket, and Judge Kaplan would soon shut him down. But for now it was a stand-off: E. Jean Carroll with Robbie Kaplan at the front table, E. Jean staring straight ahead, and Trump in his red tie two table behind, looking at the prospective jurors when they came in.

The voir dire was proceeding routinely until Judge Kaplan asked, Does anyone here think the 2020 election was stolen? Yes, said Juror Number 48.

Yes, said Juror Number 49, soon to answer Judge Kaplan's question about being COVID vaccinated with No, she was not. Online

some said, What about HIPPA? In the
courtroom Habba said, Sometimes the
Internet can be mean. But what would it
mean, this second trial on damages,
shoehorned in between the Iowa caucus and
the New Hampshire primary? Kurt tried to
tweet out every word.

He put a link on Threads, only to be told,
Some of us here will never go back to that
hell site. This was America 2024: separate
worlds, two views of the very same thing.
And Kurt tried to serve it up, what was
actually said.

Last time he'd gone up to Bergdorf Goodman,
up to the sixth floor under the eyes of the
guards. This, where? Frozen New
Hampshire? Judge Engoran's courtroom one
block west? South to E. Jean Prettyman by
the DC Mall, or further down to Georgia or
Fort Pierce? The Trump Trial were

proliferating and beginning to blot out all others. And Kurt was on the case(s)

* * *

Online there were calls for sanctions against Habba. But in the courthouse the reviews were more nuanced. This attack dog style just might work, or at least mitigate. Where was the financial damage? Kurt Wheelock had liked the Horrible Men book, but few others had. The Cut had been the payday, E. Jean's Q factor was up. It seemed cruel or right wing to note it. But what would the jurors see?

* * *

II. 1/16-17/24

Life, sure, but Jean could always leave
Amid the ghosts of horny boys
Debrief, by motel microwave
A sodden song of songs.

But one malefactor glowed
Oranger than the others

And The Cut of course they ate it up
An Annie's Burrito, bean and cheese.

In the hours after the slice of The Cut
The vast red-hatted army
Ran their reviews on Rumble
She could not look away

So now a second reckoning
This time with Orange Man present
Jurors urged to use false names
To kill the red-tied snake.

III. Jury Selection

And so it began:

OK - Carroll v. Trump 2d trial, jury selection to start. So far E. Jean Carroll at front table - now Trump has entered the courtroom.

Trump is leaning over at defense table, whispering with one of his lawyers. E. Jean Carroll, seated at the front table, has not turned around to look at him. Still no sign of

Judge Kaplan; his deputy Andy was up front, now stepped out.

Alina Habba is leaning forward to talk to Trump, then to others of his lawyers at the middle table.

All rise!

Judge Kaplan: Before we get to the jurors, there are a few things I want to say. I trust we can agree that I will ask the whole panel whether any of them are in a position where they cannot be fair, and I'll excuse those who say yes. Anyone have a problem? No. No.

Judge Kaplan: Each party, Ms. Carroll and Mr. Trump, is now prohibited from trying to communicate to any juror, unless the court and the other side have been advised, and the court has given permission. No party can object except through their lawyers

Judge Kaplan: The Court has issued restrictions... Ms. Habba have you advised Mr. Trump of them? Habba: We have issues with them we'd like to address. Judge Kaplan:

I'll hear you briefly, but that's the way it's going to be. 2d Trump lawyer: We have an appeal

2d Trump lawyer: Being here, we have forfeited our right to appeal to the Supreme Court --

Judge Kaplan: Overruled.

2d Trump lawyer: The decision in the first case is on appeal, we preserve the right --

Judge Kaplan: Overruled.

2d Trump lawyer: The Court has found that admitting the Anderson Cooper is overly prejudicial to Ms. Carroll --

Judge Kaplan: I said a lot more than that. 2d Trump lawyer: We don't know if the other 2 women will testify. We tried to include an expert...

2d Trump lawyer: The rulings in the last 72 hours prohibit us-

Judge Kaplan: Overruled.

Habba: Thanks, Michael. Your Honor, how are we supposed to prepare? Judge Kaplan: You have a witness list.

Habba: Your order did not address it. Judge Kaplan: I won't rule yet   Judge Kaplan: In my courtroom, when the ruling is made, that's the end. Habba: What about the funeral on Thursday? I've never seen someone have to choose between being at a trial being sued for millions of dollars. My client flew through the night to be here

Judge Kaplan: You asked for a week and I denied it. I have said if you rest your case by Thursday, he need not be here. We will continue the case to the next Monday. That's the allowance I am going to make. The repetition is not accomplishing anything

Habba: I would like to proceeding today and tomorrow, and not Thursday.

Judge Kaplan: I have ruled.

2d Trump lawyer: It is unnecessary to gag both parties during the trial. You can tell the jurors not to read media.

Judge Kaplan: There is no gag order. 2d Trump lawyer: So the parties are free to talk about the trial?

Judge Kaplan: Not in this courtroom or to the jurors.

Habba: You've made your mind up. On Anderson Cooper, you've ruled we can't play what she said about rape being [seen by some as] sexy

Judge Kaplan: I will rule as the issues arise. Ms. Kaplan, how long will your case take? Roberta Kaplan: Two, two and a half.

Judge Kaplan: And Ms. Habba? Putting aside if Mr. Trump testifies. Habba: Putting that aside, a day, day and a half. Carol Martin and...

Habba: Then Mr. Trump, it would depend if the other two testify. I see you think it's funny -- Judge Kaplan: It's not funny. You want to call Martin, but they shouldn't? Habba: We should get to call her first.

Carroll's 2d lawyer: We don't think she has relevance

Judge Kaplan: You can cross her. Is the jury pool not ready?

2d Carroll lawyer: Ms. Martin was cross examined last time on her views of Mr. Trump. That's not permissible here.

Judge Kaplan: I'll deal with his as it arises. We'll take a recess Thread will continue

Interim update: Trump is still at the defense table waiting, with Judge Kaplan out of the courtroom and the prospective jurors not yet in. E. Jean Carroll is still in the courtroom too, at the front table.

OK, the judge is back. Judge Kaplan: Let's begin seating the prospective jurors. [Trump, Carroll and their lawyers all standing and waiting as prospects file into the jury box]

[Now the gallery benches are filled with prospective jurors, too.]

Courtroom deputy Andy: Would all jurors please rise and raise your right hands at this time? Will you answer with the truth, the whole truth and nothing but the truth so help you God?

Judge Kaplan: This case is between a writer and advice columnist E. Jean Carroll and former president Donald J. Trump. We expect the case to take 3 to 5 days of trial. We will sit today through all or part of Thursday, then Monday.

Judge Kaplan: We need to find a panel that is willing and able to decide this case fairly. Both parties have a right to excuse a limited number of jurors without giving any reason. I don't want to embarrass anyone. I can hear you at the sidebar. Judge Kaplan: You will be anonymous.

Tomorrow those selected, you will be picked up at locations and be driven into the underground garage. I suggest that you consider whether it would be a good idea to use a name other than your own - so other jurors don't know

Judge Kaplan: This is for your own protection. This case has attracted media attention in the past and will, it seems, this time. We want you protected for harassment and invasions of your privacy. No cell phones, no posting of anything on the Internet, no reading

Judge Kaplan: Don't tell your family members and loved ones that you are on this case... Ms. Carroll sued Mr. Trump for defamation in statements he made in June 2019 after she accused him of having sexually assaulted her in the mid-1990s

Judge Kaplan: Mr. Trump denied knowing her and said she only made the accusation in order to sell a book. For purposes on this trial, it has been determined already that Mr. Trump did sexually assault Ms. Carroll, the jury does not need to decide that.

Judge Kaplan: Mr. Trump contends that Ms. Carroll is entitled to only nominal damages, and no punitive damages. I need to ask you: if the answer is Yes, please raise your hand or stand up. Would you be unable to give both sides a fair trial?

Judge Kaplan: Anyone in the jury box say Yes, unable? In the jury box, Seat 10, Number 20. And in the back, the man with the open collar? Number 7. Thank you. Number 9? Seat 40. Thank you, be seated. Those three, Jurors 20, 40 and 41, you are excused

Judge Kaplan: OK, next group of questions - again if the answer is Yes, raise your hand or stand up. Does anyone personally know Ms. Carroll or her family? No affirmative response. Anyone seen anything about her that would make it hard to be fair? No affirmative

Judge Kaplan: Anyone had dealing with Ms. Carroll's law firm?

Prospective juror: I worked with them pro bono on marriage equality issues.

Judge Kaplan: OK. Anyone personally know Mr. Trump or his family? No affirmative response. Anyone work for him? Lady in back? Prospective juror: In 2017 I worked for Ivanka Trump's company. Judge Kaplan: Could you be fair?

Prospective juror: Yes. Judge Kaplan: Gentleman? Number 36? 36: I was a US Navy Officer. Judge Kaplan: Would that impact your fairness? 36: No Sir.

Prospective juror 69: My father's moving company, we were the movers for the Trump companies when they did the buildings on the West Side. Judge Kaplan: Could you be fair? 69: Yes. J

Judge Kaplan: Has anyone volunteered for Mr. Trump or campaign? Prospective juror: I spoke at the White House. We do policy advocacy work. Judge Kaplan: Did you meet Mr. Trump?

Prospective juror: Only indirectly. Judge Kaplan: Could you be fair?

Prospect: Yes

Judge Kaplan: Does anyone know Ms. Habba? No affirmative response. You may hear testimony from or about, Ms. Crowley?

Crowley: Bergdoft, Humphreys, Carol Martin, Robbie Myers Habba: Ms. Martin is not on that list, correct? Judge Kaplan: That was unnecessary

Prospective juror 27: I know Robbie Myers, editor of Elle, I have my own company. Judge Kaplan: Could you be fair? 27: Yes.

Judge Kaplan: Have you read seen or heard anything about this case? In the jury box, seats 1, 9, 13, 14, 15, 17 and 18

Judge Kaplan: Would this make you unable to be fair? No affirmative response. In the back? Andy could you read out the numbers?

Andy: Seat 20, Number 27; Seat 21, Juror 3; Seat 24, 58; Seat 25, 16; Seat 26, 42; Seat 27, 1; Seat 28, 70; Seat 29, 79; Seat 30, 68

Judge Kaplan: For those in the back, stand again if anything you've read seen or heard would make fairness impossible. No affirmative response. I'm reminded, to ask Ms. Habba about her witnesses & places.

Habba: President Trump and the other name was already said

Judge Kaplan: Have you heard about the previous case, sometimes called Carroll II? No affirmative response. Raise your hand if you are registered to vote. Number 34 are you enrolled in a political party? Yes. Number 56?

Response: No I am not.

Judge Kaplan: Raise your hand if you voted in the 2020 Presidential election... All but 2. Let the lawyers make notes. Did you vote in 2016 and/or 2020? Both. Both. Both. Only

2020 (one says, then another) Last row: Both, Both.

 Judge Kaplan: Has anyone contributed to Mr. Trump or his campaigns or PACs supporting him?

Voice: Yes. And I have family members who donated.

 Judge Kaplan: How about supporting a candidate who Mr. Trump supported? No affirmative response.

Judge Kaplan: How about support to campaigns of Barrack Obama, Hillary Clinton or Joe Biden? Hands can go down.

Number 3: For Joe Biden...

 Judge Kaplan: Anyone back on the left gone to a rally for Mr. Trump?

68: Yes. Judge Kaplan: Anyone think the 2020 election was stolen? Voices: "68." Then also "69."

Judge Kaplan: Unable to be fair? No affirmative response. Have you been a member of Redneck Revolt? Proud Boys? Oath Keepers? KKK? Thin Blue Line? Trump Supporters of NY? No.

Judge Kaplan: Have you ever posted on Truth Social or Rumble? No affirmative response. Have you seen any posts about Ms. Carroll? 18/63: Yes.

Judge Kaplan: Has anyone seen allegations of sexual misconduct by Mr. Trump? Stand up. Number 3: In newspapers. 27: And TV

Judge Kaplan: Has anyone seen news of criminal indictments of Mr. Trump? Lot of hands. Could anything make you unfair? Number 18 / 63. Anyone else? Shall I excuse 63? Yes. On consent. Please give your card to Andy. Has anyone regularly read Ask E. Jean? No

Judge Kaplan: Anyone watched The Apprentice? Enough time lawyers? Anything you've seen make you unfair? No affirmative response. Formed any views on the credibility of Mr. Trump or Ms. Carroll that you could not put aside? No affirmative response.

 Judge Kaplan: Anyone believe presidential immunity covers this case? It does not - he can be sued. No affirmative response. For this trial, it has been determined Mr. Trump sexually assaults Ms. Carroll, and he defamed her. Anyone can't accept that? No affirmative answer

Judge Kaplan: Anyone accused of, or accusing of, unwanted touching or abuse? Lady in the back?

A: I'm fine answering your question. My ex-spouse was accused.

Judge Kaplan: Were you the accuser? A: No. I can be fair. Judge Kaplan: I instruct jurors not to discuss the case on social media. Could anyone not resist the temptation? No affirmative response. Hearing or vision problem? No affirmative response. Anyone not speak English? No affirmative response.

Judge Kaplan: Anyone been a party to a civil lawsuit? 42 (male) - Yes, landlord tenant cases, family members. Judge Kaplan: Could you be fair? 42: Yes.

Female prospective juror: A suit against my co-op board. I could be fair. Judge Kaplan: Anyone serve on a jury? Female prospective juror: A malpractice suit in White Plains. Another: Hung jury in Baltimore City.

Man: A jury for sexual assault. It arrived at a decision. NY Supreme in the late 90s. Juror 1: Three juries, all with verdicts 73: I served on a jury in White Plains regarding something like this.

Judge Kaplan: What do you mean by that? 73: It was about writers. Something about not being available for the person. Assistant. Judge Kaplan: Thank you. Female: Robbery and cold case

Judge Kaplan: Anyone not vaccinated against COVID? Please tell me your name-- 69: My name? Judge Kaplan: Pardon me.

Judge Kaplan: Counsel, please approach. [Whispered sidebar - will 69 and 68 be bounded by Team Carroll? Thread will continue below]

They're back. Judge Kaplan: Juror 3, you said you did something for or with Mr. Biden. What was it? 3: I made phone calls. A phone bank.

Judge Kaplan: Campaigns can, if they have enough money, hire people. Were you hired? 3: I was a volunteer.

Judge Kaplan: Anyone feel Mr. Trump is being treated unfairly by the court system? Please stand up. Oh, Number 68 in the back of the room. And in jury box, 29 in Seat 8. OK, we'll take a morning break - then come back for a few more questions

They're back. Judge Kaplan: Here's the time we find out a little more about you folks. Andy, do you want to get the microphone? Let me tell you what the questions are: How old are you - that's optional - what county, education, what do you do for a living

Judge Kaplan: your kids if any, and media. Juror: I've lived in The Bronx for 60 years. One child works in finance, the other sells time. I'm a retired MTA track supervisor. I watch Channel 7 at 6 o'clock. 56 (female) I was born in Germany. I have two children.

56: I worked for the German School of New York. I haven't looked at the news for the last year, I learn about history, colonization to the present. And about Germany. Judge Kaplan: Andy, can we crack up the volume. 28 (male) I do property management, Facebook

Voice: I'm 58, I live in Westchester. I work in cyber security sales. Son in ROTC. NY Times. Male: I'm 40, I moved to Manhattan in 2009, before that Barcelona where I'm from. Spanish newspapers. 30 (male) Software engineer. Girlfriend in NJ. I scan news

Voice (female) I run large scale operations at a university. Judge Kaplan: Operations of what? Juror: Student center. 38 (male) High school, I work in Westchester for Low Voltage. It's just a job I do. My fiancée works at a bank. We moved to Queens. TikTok

Voice (female) You can guess my age. My oldest is a litigator, my younger is in law school. WSJ. Juror 29 (female) I'm 60 and teach in Westchester. 3 kids, 1 in the Army, another in finance. News all over. Juror 6 (male) I'm 46, a doctor, NYT.

32 (female) I'm 68, I have a degree in playwriting. Voice (female) I work in underserved communities. NY Mag

66 (female) I'm 37, I lived in Miami, I'm a publicist for Big Tech. Newspapers. 82 (male) Therapist, I live in Westchester for 17 years, news from YouTube

Juror 10 (male) I'm 40, no kids. Post production for TV shows. 69 (female) I live in Westchester, I am a diversity officer for a large communications union, I'm a work place investigator. Juror 27 (female) Native Manhattanite. I own my own communications firm

Juror 3 (female) Westchester, I work in my town library. My children are graphic designers. Pod Save America.

Judge Kaplan: Let me have that one again - God Save America? 3: Pod. 4 (female) Manhattan, I am a costume designer. 36 (male) I am 36, Tribeca, banker

58 (female) I am 40, Westchester. 2 kids, I have a Masters, Board of Ed 68 (male) I grew up in British Columbia, corporate lawyer at a multinational. Aggregators like Real Clear Politics.

79 (male) Westchester, 2 kids, my last job was in streaming media

70 (female) I'm a violinist. Print media and the radio. Juror 1 (female) Native New York, single, I teach science. Juror 42 (male) I'm a prosecutor, now I live in Manhattan. Juror 16

(female) Originally from Israel. I work for a tech company. I have an MBA.

Voice (male) I work in marketing, as do my sons. I log into my email, I scan Yahoo newsfeed. Juror 2: Putnam County. Pharmaceutical, I'm a scientist. Juror 5 (female) I have a BFA in musical theater. I am single, NYT and social media Juror 73 (female) Retired

Juror 85 (male) I'm a performer, I'm between jobs. BFA, Internet outlets. Juror 61 (male) Work at a big bank, Manhattan, social media. Juror 45 (Male) I'm from Azerbaijan, Baku Judge Kaplan: Slower. 45: US for 28 years, work at hospital, Euro News on TV

Voice (male) I live in the Bronx and work at Montefiore Hospital, I watch Fox and Channel 12 Voice (male) My husband and I live in Manhattan. Juror 75 (female) retired teacher, I live in The Bronx.

Judge Kaplan: Juror 11, did you say you live in Queens? When did you get your jury notice? 11 (male) I used to live in Yonkers. Judge Kaplan: Counsel, may I see you at sidebar? They've back. Judge Kaplan: Andy, please read out the jurors.

Andy: Juror 34 is 1; 56 is 2; 28 is 3; 21 is 4, 23 is 5, 6 is 6 (what are the odds, someone says), 66 is 7, 82 is 8 and 10 is 9. Judge Kaplan: We're resume at 3 pm with openings. Thread will continue

OK, they're back - except, Trump is not at the defense table. A 3d of his lawyers starts speaking and -- Judge Kaplan: Are you a member of the bar of this court? 3d lawyer: No, I'm a member of the New York State bar Judge Kaplan: Please sit down. Jury entering!

Judge Kaplan: The plaintiff has the burden to make the scales tip - but this is not proof beyond a reasonable doubt, put that out of your mind. A magazine published an excerpt including Ms. Carroll's account of being sexually assaulted by Mr. Trump in Bergdorf's

Judge Kaplan: Mr. Trump denied knowing Ms. Carroll, and said she made it up for an improper purpose. There has been a prior jury decision, some of which is binding on you: Mr. Trump in fact sexually abused Ms. Carroll by inserting his finger into her v*gina

Judge Kaplan: Mr. Trump's false statements were defamatory. You will decide if he should pay punitive damages... You shall not use social media, including Twitter now X. I expect you will tell me if another juror does. Try not to form an opinion until the end

IV. Carroll's Opening

Judge Kaplan: Now, opening statements. Plaintiff?

Carroll's Shawn Crowley: In the Spring of 1996, Donald Trump sexually assaulted E. Jean Carroll. That's a fact. It has been proven. A jury sitting in the same seats as you found that it happened. Why are we here?

Carroll's Crowley: She came forward in June 2019. Donald Trump said he never met her, that she just made it up to make money. He was President, he used the world's biggest microphone against Ms. Carroll. He told lies. That's already been decided

Carroll's Crowley: What are you here to decide? Whether Donald Trump's defamatory statements caused her harm. And if so, how much should he pay. This trial is only about damages. She had a reputation as a writer and advice columnist. He unleashed his followers

Carroll's Crowley: You'll see the threatening messages she received. She lives every day in fear from the threats she gets from his followers online. How much money will it take to make him stop? He didn't stop in 2019. He did it in October 2022. And today he lies

Carroll's Crowley: Today as Donald Trump campaigns for president he continues to defame Ms. Carroll. We are proud to represent her. You'll hear from the former editor of Elle.

Carroll's Crowley: Ms. Carroll is going to tell you she grew up in Indiana, and submitted her first article at 12. She was a beauty pageant queen. She wrote for SNL, then Ask E. Jean for Elle. Then Donald Trump sexually assaulted her. In Bergdorf's.

Carroll's Crowley: They had met at a party, with their then spouses. Here is a photo [John Johnson, Ivana Trump] In 2017 she took a road trip, to write a book, listening to women about men. It became a memoir, and NY Magazine published an excerpt.

Carroll's Crowley: Donald Trump over the course of four days issued baseless attacks. On June 21, 2019 then President Trump claimed he never met Ms. Carroll in his life. He called it a disgrace. He threatened her, saying People should pay dearly for making it up

Carroll's Crowley: Four days later he lied again-- Trump's 2d lawyer: Objection. No damages are being sought for that. Judge Kaplan: But it is relevant to another issue, Mr. Madaio, and you know that.

Carroll's Crowley: Suddenly Ms. Carroll was branded a fraud

Carroll's Crowley: He spoke from the White House. And many believed him and they went after Ms. Carroll. They bombarded him with threatening tweets. Within minutes, people amplified Mr. Trump, on Facebook and Twitter. They called her a liar

Carroll's Crowley: Donald Trump's attacks have her living her life in fear. And they ruined her professional reputation. You'll hear from Robbie Myers of Elle... She went from a respected columnist to being viewed as a political operative. Her dream was shattered

Carroll's Crowley: In October 2022 Donald Trump told his followers that her story is a con job and a hoax. She sued him again, including for the sexual assault under the New York State law. That suit moved faster, in a two-week trial last spring.

Carroll's Crowley: The jury found assault and defamation. But the day after, Donald Trump went on CNN and called her a liar, and a wack job. He lies, even today. You'll hear that as Donald Trump faces trial, he keeps doing it. He sat here this morning and posted

Carroll's Crowley: He posted 22 times today. As he runs for president, he continues to defame her. You'll be asked to decide how much money he should have to pay, to ensure that he never defames her again. It's time to hold Donald Trump accountable

Carroll's Crowley: It's to make Donald Trump pay, dearly.

V. Trump's Habba, Opening

Judge Kaplan: Thank you. Ms. Habba?

Alina Habba: I represent former president Donald J. Trump. This is about two statements. Two. The other side will attempt to paint Ms. Carroll as losing everything

Habba: President Trump defended himself when publicly accused -- Carroll's lawyer: Objection, Your Honor! Judge Kaplan: Don't go much further. Habba: Her career has prospered. She has been thrust back into the limelight like she always wanted

Habba: She has to prove that she actually suffered harm, attributable to two statements. Two. She will allege two types of harm, compensatory and punitive... This case is about defamation, not assault. You're not here to make her whole from that.

Habba: These days, the Internet always something to say and it's not always nice. She waited 30 years, when she was making less-- Carroll's lawyer: Objection! Judge Kaplan: Basis? Carroll's lawyer: "She waited 30 years" Judge: Overruled

Habba: They just said, He unleashed his followers. But before he spoke her name she was being denounced as a liar. Now she wants President Trump to pay for the mean tweets. Ms. Carroll enjoyed controversial discussions in the public. She liked that

Habba: She wrote about "frigid women." And "a dog in heat... Men Catching Made Easy, Mr. Right, Right Now." And "What Do We Need Men For"? These books featured her face on the cover. She moved from Montana to NY because the quiet life didn't suit her

Habba: Her career was dwindling in 2014. She needed a spark. Even this book was not met with critical acclaim. Her interviews were about Donald Trump, not the book. Even her own close friends thought her head was getting too big

Habba: It is no secret that if you speak about President Trump you will elicit reactions, positive and negative. Should he foot the bill? The evidence I will show you will show you that Ms. Carroll's conduct has caused this media frenzy. She chose New York Magazine

Habba: If you make explosive allegations against a sitting president, any sitting president, you will spark a reaction. There were scores of tweets directed at her in the five hours after she posted her story in The Cut, which paid her, before any Trump statement

Habba: She was fully enjoying the attention. We will ask Ms. Carroll to confirm that she felt she was in a cocoon of love after the publication. She has become an advocate, this has become part of her identity because that was her plan. She will continue

Habba: She has gone on podcasts she couldn't possibly have been on.. to increase her public profile. Duty to minimize the effects, it's not my client's duty, it's hers. She spread the message far and wide. She was the catalyst of her own harm.

Habba: This is about mean tweet from Twitter trolls. She has to show they are from my client's two statements. She went on TV. Again and again and again. Duty to mitigate. Ms. Carroll has made Trump the focal point of her new identity

Habba: She has been monetizing her brand for years, she had plans to continue doing so. Her social circle has changed. She is widely regarded as an anti-Trump person, she hands out with Mary Trump, a vocal critic of her uncle. A new book, a romance, is planned

Habba: She is friends with Kathy Griffin, shown her - I would not allow my child to post it, holding a replica of President Trump's severed head. She got what she wanted. It's up to you now. See through this charade - tell her, just as they said, it is enough

Habba: She craves fame and has, long before Trump. They have to be able to prove to you that the harm is because of those two statements that he said, nothing else. They will not be able to do that. Their expert has never executed a reputation repair campaign

Habba: They want President Trump to pay her money to pay social media influencers to post messages. It is severely flawed, I will walk you through it. Their expert ignored any positive she has experienced. Their expert left out whatever doesn't serve their case

Habba: So why are we here? Your task is to determine, the judge will articulate what he wants you to determine- Judge Kaplan: The judge will NOT articulate what to determine, only the law Habba: I was trying to avoid an objection Judge Kaplan: You've done it again

Habba: She wants another award. Your job is to give her more money. But regardless of a few mean tweets, she has more famous than ever before. They cannot fulfil their burden. Thank you for your time. Judge Kaplan: We'll resume tomorrow. Counsel, remain

[Jury exits

Judge Kaplan: Anything else? No? OK I will see you tomorrow. All rise

VI.   Who Owns This Stage?

E. Jean was in a hotel room
So small there was no table there.
When in The Cut, they fingered Trump
For assault with what in time turned out
To be his finger.

A Tsunami of Hate
Mean tweets and Instagram
No more questions to E. Jean
Death threats and cocoon of love.

Dissected now, how much it's worth
The Orange Man loudly says a witch hunt
Kaplan steps to play his role
In the Orange Man's drama...
Who owns this stage?

VII. Carroll on the Witness Stand

LITERARY SDNY, Jan 17 – E. Jean Carroll took the witness stand and now Trump, three tables back, faced her. The direct examination was methodical.

She had been in a small hotel room over 10th Avenue in Manhattan when what she called the wave of hate and slime rose up, splashing from the laptop she set up on a board.

There was a death threat, she said, and the room's window was open. She deleted it, and more. She did not sleep. Then she told her friend online that she was fine as wine.

At the break her second lawyer Shawn Crowley asked Judge Kaplan to act on what she called Trump's loud stage whispers, like "It's true" when a video of him in the Buckeye State was played, and "It's a witch hunt."

Judge Kaplan obliged, telling Trump that his right to be present at his trial could be forfeited by disruptive behavior. Journalists ran to write their stories, but Kurt Wheelock had already tweeted his.

Returning to the courtroom Trump's second lawyer asked that Judge Kaplan recuse himself, that Shawn Crowley had been his law clerk. Was it like the Engoran / Lisa G interplay just one block west? The cross began--

* * *

Online the tsunami of negative reviews this time was directed at Alina Habba. Some wrote, had she gone to Trump University? Learned her law from Law & Order? But perhaps there was a method to her madness, to draw objections that Judge Kaplan would sustain, so that her client could use it. Most litigants try to win a trial. But perhaps the Orange Man was playing a different game. And was Judge Kaplan playing into it? Would Trump actually testify and be cross examined on Monday? Kurt Wheelock would be there.

Blow by Blow, Play by Play

OK- Day 2 of Carroll v. Trump 2d trial. Trump has entered the courtroom, seated in red tie at defense table with Alina Habba. Carroll will be the witness.

All rise! Judge Kaplan: The delay this morning was caused by a transportation problem. Before the jury comes in, I have the following questions of law after yesterday's defense opening. Is mitigation of damages an affirmative defense? Is it waived? Judge Kaplan: Is the defense even applicable to a defamation case? If so, which side has the burden of proof, and what must be proved to satisfy that burden. There is a NY Court of Appeals case, it is 226 NY1, Sun Printing - and App Div in Caine, find it

Habba: I would like to address what your Honor is recommending in writing overnight

- you're proposing an instruction, right? Judge Kaplan: I want briefs on Friday before 4pm.

Habba: My client & I wish to point out Ms. Carroll can sit in front of jurors every day

Habba: But my client has to choose between attending his mother in law's funeral --

Judge Kaplan: I have ruled. Sit down. Habba: I don't like to be spoken to that why. Please refrain. I am asking for an adjournment for a funeral.

Judge Kaplan: Denied. Sit down. Judge Kaplan: Bring in the jury. Robbie Kaplan (RK): Plaintiff calls E. Jean Carroll. RK: Where do you live? Carroll: In upstate NY in the mountains, in a small cabin. RK: Why are you here? Carroll: Donald Trump abused then defamed me and shattered my reputation

Roberta Kaplan: Has Mr. Trump continued to lie about you?

Carroll: He lied Sunday, and yesterday. Habba: Objection - non responsive, and not at issue here. Judge Kaplan: Certainly relevant to damages. Overruled.

RK: How was your reputation shattered?

Carroll: Yesterday on Twitter I saw, Hey lady, you're a fraud. Previously I was a columnist. Now I'm known as a wack job. People don't write to an advice columnist that's being attacked like this.

RK: In the first case, what were your claims? Carroll: Assault and defamation. RK: When was the assault? Carroll: 1996. RK: How long did the trial last? Carroll: 2 weeks. RK: Who cross examined you?

Carroll: Joe Tacopina

Habba: Objection   Judge Kaplan: Sustained.

RK: Where did you grow up? Carroll: Indiana. My mother was a volunteer for the Republican Party

Habba: Objection, relevance. Judge Kaplan: Background. Habba: You ruled no politics

Judge Kaplan: Fair enough. RK: How did your parents raise you? Carroll: Small school house. They had 2 rules: smile and look on the bright side. I wanted to be a writer.

RK: Where'd you go to college? Carroll: Indiana University. I was a cheerleader. Carroll: I was nominated for a beauty pageant. Another Trump lawyer: Objection

Judge Kaplan: Who said that? This is not tag team.

RK: How did you become a writer?

Carroll: After 20 years of negativity, I got my first piece accepted at age 46. I taught gym in Idaho

Carroll: I was found in the slush pile at Esquire. Then other doors opened. I wrote for Rolling Stone, New York

RK: Did you move to New York City?
Carroll: In 1980 or 1981. I said, I love it here. And I stayed.

RK: How'd you become an advice columnist? Carroll: Elle gave me a column in 1993. People ask questions, my answers were published. Ask E Jean.

RK: What is this photo? Carroll: This is me [in a loosely tied tie] Dec 1995

RK: What kind of questions did you get? Carroll: The comedy and drama of life. Mostly, How do I get my husband to take my showers? And, How do I get my wife to let me get back in bed and off the couch. I had 80% women, 20% men. I broke with the past

Carroll: I was all about taking action. Lead an adventurous life. It was light hearted - but deeply serious. I had a TV show too. RK: When?

Carroll: 1994 to 1996, then the channel I was on became MSNBC. My channel was started by Roger Ailes. RK: Did you appear on other TV shows?

Carroll: Yes, GMA, The Bill Maher Show, Anderson Cooper, the shows that were on every day. I could be slotted in for four minutes RK: How often were you on TV?

Carroll: Often

Habba: Objection - too broad

RK: Most recently? Carroll: Today Show, weekly, 2015 to 2016. RK: Have you written books? Carroll: Five. A bio of Hunter Thompson. A book of essays. A memoir.

RK: This is "Female Difficulties." Forgive me, but it looks a little dated. Carroll: It's from 1983

RK: Put up the Hunter S. Thompson biography.

Carroll: He's the astonish journalist. I wrote it between 1991 and 1992, it was published in 1993. It was extremely well reviewed. The reviewers were all journalists and they all loved Hunter.

RK: And this book?

Carroll: It's about what women think --
Habba: Objection, vague. What women think --

Judge Kaplan: Ms. Habba, when you speak in this courtroom or any other courtroom you'll stand up

Carroll: Women were very blunt, in Alabama and Arkansas & Ohio - they were thrilled to talk to a journalist. RK: When did you start writing it? Carroll: 2017. It was published in 2019. RK: Was Donald Trump initially on your list?

Carroll: No. But I was overwhelmed

RK: What did you say about Mr. Trump in that book? Carroll: That we met outside of Bergdorf's... He asked me to help buy a gift. We went to the lingerie department

Judge Kaplan: Ms. Habba?

Habba: Objection. Already determined. RK: How many pages are about Mr. Trump?

Carroll: Nine. Ms. Kaplan, may I have my glasses? They're in my purse. Good luck finding them in that bag

Habba: I object. This goes to the underlying facts.

RK: We can redact it further. They've had this a long time

Judge Kaplan: I'm advised that the version on the screen is not redacted. RK: This is what Mr. Trump reacted to.

Judge Kaplan: Ms. Habba, what about that? Habba: The president denied an allegation on the White House lawn from a reporter.

Habba: We can't ask her about the other men, that she claimed assaulted her. Judge Kaplan: I don't get what you said but I'm going to sustain it anyway.

Habba: Move to strike. Judge Kaplan: To strike what? Madaio: Ms. Kaplan read it.

Judge Kaplan: Mr. Madaio...

RK: What an excerpt published?

Carroll: June 21, 2019 in New York Magazine. RK: What time of day?

Carroll: The NYT was going to publish an article about the book, that caused NY Magazine to rush it out on Friday, in the afternoon. They jumped the gun

RK: Did the excerpt include the assault by Donald Trump? Carroll: yes.

RK: Yesterday Ms. Habba talked about a five-hour interval. Did the except include a denial? Carroll: Yes, a denial from the White House Habba: She is waiving the ability for me to cross examine

 RK: Had you told anyone publicly the story about Mr. Trump?

Carroll: No.

RK: Did it factor in, that he was President? Carroll: Yes. I went ahead and did it. RK: Did you expect him to respond? Carroll: I thought he'd say it was consensual.

RK: Is that what he did? Carroll: No. He said my false accusation damaged the real victims of sexual assault, that is a lie

Habba: Objection

 Judge Kaplan: On what ground? In one word

Habba: She is not a lawyer

Judge Kaplan: Overruled

RK: Have you paid dearly? Carroll: Just about as dearly as it is possible to pay.

 RK: What is this document?

Carroll: An announcement by the Office of the Press Secretary. RK: Move to admit.

Judge Kaplan: Received. Carroll: He said that numerous women had been paid to make false accusations about him and that these women did very well --

Habba: Objection

Judge Kaplan: Overruled.

Carroll: It was untrue. I was not paid. RK: What about paying dearly? Carroll: He said people like me should tread carefully -

Habba: Objection

Judge Kaplan: Overruled. RK: What is the context of these statements by Mr. Trump? Carroll: He's on his way to the helicopter, questions from journalists

 RK: What's this from The Hill?

Carroll: It's partially about me.

Habba: Objection. It's not part of this case.

 Judge Kaplan: Overruled...Jurors, this statement is not part of the application for damages.

RK: What's new here? Carroll: It said, I'm not his type

Carroll: He said, I'm not his type. Meaning, I'm too ugly-

Habba: Objection - speculation.

Judge Kaplan: Overruled. You can cross examine. Carroll: The president called me a liar 26 times. It ended the world I had been living in. I'm in a new world.

RK: What next? Carroll: I was attacked. On Twitter. On Facebook. It was a new world.

RK: What is this? Carroll: A Facebook chat, directed to me.

RK: Do you know the author? Carroll: No. It was June 21, 2019, at 6:09 pm RK: What is UCT? Carroll: Universal time code

RK: What is this? Carroll: A message on Facebook. The Monday, June 24, 2019.

RK: What does this person say?

Carroll: He talked about how ashamed I should be, I made it harder for the true victims of abuse.

RK: Did Donald Trump say that? Carroll: Yes. RK: How often do you receive such messages? Carroll: Sometimes 100s a day. RK: What are the themes?

Carroll: That, You are a liar... You hurt victims... You are ugly. Those are first three.

RK: And your motivations? Habba: Objection. We were ordered not to discuss

Judge Kaplan: Sidebar [Whispered sidebar ensues, then they're back]

RK: Let's start with messages calling you a liar. Carroll: This is a Facebook chat. She says, She was not going to ask me for advice.

RK: This asks how much George Soros paid you. Who is he?

Carroll: A rich old man.

RK: Did you pay you? Carroll: No. RK: Do you know anyone at the DNC? Carroll: No. Habba: I will be addressing this on cross

Judge Kaplan: We'll see. I don't need announcements

Judge Kaplan: I make the rulings here.

Habba: I was just --

Judge Kaplan: Sit down.

RK: How many requests for advice did you get per month?

Carroll: Two hundred a month. Now only eight.

RK: Is this a good time for a morning break?
Judge Kaplan: Yes. 15 minutes.

With jury out Carroll's Shawn Crowley: Ms. Habba has twice now mentioned other men - now she's brought up that Ms. Carroll received funding for this case. That was improper. And Mr. Trump has been loudly saying, *She got her memory back*

Judge Kaplan: Ms. Habba? Habba: They asked her if she had funding, she said no. We know that she had funding.

Judge Kaplan: What about Mr. Trump being vocal in the presence of the jury?

Carroll's Shawn Crowley: We asked about funding from George Soros, not for this lawsuit

Habba: It's Reid Hoffman

Judge Kaplan: I'll consider what you said. [Leaves bench. The "Trump vocalization" issue not addressed. Yet? Thread will continue.

They're back.

Judge Kaplan: Before the jury comes in, I'm just going to ask that Mr. Trump take special care to lower his voice when conferring with counsel so that the jury doesn't overhear it. Jury entering!

 [Now Trump whispering directly into Habba's ear]

RK: Ms. Carroll, what is this?

Carroll: My tweet before Mr. Trump's statement. My tweet was about taking a road trip. And this reply hits all the high spot - saying I'm psychologically messed up. And that's ugly and should avoid a mirror. I know I'm old but

RK: Did any of the messages you received accuse you of being promiscuous?

Carroll: Yes. This email was sent to me, and my publisher and my agent. It made me feel horrible.

RK: Did you receive some even more upsetting?

Carroll: They threatened to kill me

RK: How many threatened violence? Carroll: Hundreds.

RK: What was the first time?

Carroll: Around 11:30 that night, I was in a cheap hotel on 10th Avenue. The room was small, there was no desk, just a board you flapped down - I went to Twitter for breaking news

 Carroll: On Twitter I saw, You lying scumbag - so I went to my Ask E Jean website, looking for support - there was a lovely email saying You Go Girl but the next one, I thought I was going to get shot. I couldn't get the curtain closed

Carroll: There was a message with a photo of a woman who had obviously been murdered, there was blood on her neck-

Habba: Objection, inflammatory

Judge Kaplan: Sustained. Carroll: I hit delete, delete. I couldn't help myself. I went back to Twitter

RK: Did you sleep a lot that night? Carroll: No, because of the window. I didn't sleep until six or seven in the morning.

RK: What is this?

Carroll: A Facebook message to me... "Dishonest treasonous lemmings," it describes how I should die.

RK: Prior to June 2019 had any reader ever accused you of being a pedophile, or a Satan worshipping Nazi?

Carroll: No. RK: What's this? Carroll: A Facebook message, a day after last year's trial. They want me murdered, they say

[On the screen for jurors: a message incl "no lube"]

Carroll: I'm sorry that people in this courtroom have to see these images (sobs)

RK: Some of these were posted on public media sites- but the threats of violence were sent to you privately, right?

Carroll: Yes

RK: Why didn't you delete your social media accounts?

Carroll: My favorite journalists are on social media - to not be on it, as a writer, would be oblivion.

RK: Did you ever come to regret coming forward about Mr. Trump in light of these messages?

Carroll: Only momentarily. I'm glad I took action. RK: What steps have you taken to protect yourself? Carroll: I let my pitbull off his leash. I put in an electronic fence

Carroll: I bought bullets for the gun I inherited from my father. I keep it by my bed

RK: And driving? Carroll: I pay attention to who's behind me. When I run errands, I look to see who is around. At the grocery I had a filled cart and I see a man in a brown shirt

 Carroll: Back at my home, I realized I left my groceries back at the store.

RK: Do you have personal security with you at this trial?

Carroll: Yes.

RK: Would you like more? Carroll: I can't afford it. RK: Do you tell your friends about the threats? Carroll: No. What can they do? I stay cheery.

RK: Who is Lisa Birnbach? Carroll: My friend of more than 30 years.

 RK: What did you tell her, the night in the small hotel room?

Carroll: That I was Fine as wine

RK: What's this?

Carroll: My texts with Carol Martin and her daughter. RK: Who is Carol Martin?

Carroll: The breakthrough Black newswoman. RK: You told her there were no security concerns - was that true? Carroll: I didn't want them to worry

 RK: Did you promote your book - switching gears, sorry Carroll: I did 4 TV interviews. & 4 or 5 podcasts RK: What did you talk about?

Carroll: The journalists wanted to hear about President Trump. I saw that the book was not selling - so I tried to talk about it

RK: Were you buoyant, as it said in this interview with Keziah Weir?

Carroll: That's the public E. Jean

[How Has E. Jean Carroll's Life Been Since Accusing Donald Trump? "Fabulous. Buoyant." It's been a week since the longtime advice columnist accused Donald Trump of attacking her. In a wide-ranging interview, the author discusses how she decided to go public, the support of her friends,"]

RK: What was this talking tour? Carroll: There are many tours in New York, Edgar Allan Poe Judge Kaplan: What about this tour?

Carroll: It was in front of Trump Tower

RK: When did you decide to sue?

Carroll: I was at a party with George Conway. He took me aside. He had an iPad. He explained the difference between a criminal case and a civil case. He took me through the steps. He said he could suggest an attorney

Carroll: A day later he sent me a recommendation.

RK: For whom? Carroll: For yourself, Robbie Kaplan. RK: What is this?

Carroll: A photo of us waiting to go up to your office to listen to our argument at the 2d Circuit Court of Appeals

RK: What is this? Carroll: My personal website.

RK: You're posting an article about your case - why? Carroll: Donald Trump keeps lying about me. I want people to know what is happening. RK: What's this?

Carroll: Me on Rachel Maddow

RK: During the first trial was there a hullaballoo getting in and out of the courthouse? Carroll: Yes

RK: It was said yesterday that you paid for a documentary- Habba: Objection. Judge Kaplan: On what ground?

Habba: That's not what I said. It misrepresents....

RK: Did you ever pay to have a documentary made? Carroll: No. RK: What is this?

Carroll: Something Donald Trump put on Truth Social. By then I thought I was rebuilding, I had started a new Substack -

Judge Kaplan: What did you do? Carroll: This was a statement I made about the last trial.

Habba: Objection - it's the last trial

Judge Kaplan: There are no damages being sought for this. But you may answer. Carroll: This statement by the president called me a hoax

Carroll: I thought I'd get my reputation back after winning the first trial. But Donald Trump went on TV-

Habba: Objection. This is not part of this case

Judge Kaplan: No speeches, just one word. Overruled.

RK: We got interrupted mid-answer. Carroll: He lied again

Carroll: Right after the trial he went on CNN Town Hall and lied again.

RW: What is this?

 Carroll: A Truth Social about me. A video posted by Donald Trump. Habba: We will be- Judge Kaplan: No announcements.

Habba: Objection, the whole video should be played

Judge Kaplan: No one's proposed anything else. Sit down. This is the transcript.

RK: What was this posted on Truth Social? Carroll: The day after the trial. RK: Let's play it.

[Trump: I have no idea who this woman is... the greatest witch hunt of all time]

RW: Who's the woman Mr. Trump is referring to? Carroll: Me. And Donald Trump was raising money -- Habba: Objection. That is complete speculation Judge Kaplan: The answer is stricken.

RW: Let's turn to the Town Hall - Judge Kaplan: Who much more? RW: 20 minutes. Judge Kaplan: We'll break here. 1:45.

Jury leaves.

Shawn Crowley: The defendant has been making statements we can hear. He said, *It really is a con job, it is a witch hunt.*

Remind him

Judge Kaplan: Mr. Trump has the right to be present here. That right can be forfeited if he is disruptive, which has been reported to me, and if he disregards court orders.

 Judge Kaplan: Mr. Trump, I hope I don't have to exclude you from the trial. I understand you are eager for me to do that. Control yourself. [Judge Kaplan leaves the bench]

They're back. Judge Kaplan: I understand there is an application.

Trump's lawyer Madaio: We move for recusal.

Shawn Crowley is a former law clerk, you accepted her representation... There is an atmosphere of hostility.

Judge Kaplan: Denied.

Jury entering!

Roberta Kaplan: In these four years, there have been times you've felt OK? Carroll: Oh yes. Buoyant. RK: Now let's get to the CNN Town Hall.

RK: And this disk, did you sign it? Carroll: Yes, ECJ. I followed along - the transcript is accurate.

Madaio: Objection, Your Honor.

Judge Kaplan: One lawyer per witness and you're not it. Habba: What rule is that? Judge Kaplan: My order this morning. You heard it

Judge Kaplan: OK you're had the conference and the moment is over. I can't hear you.

RK: We'll come back to this, I don't want to waste the time of the jury. [Video played,

Hawkeye State: Trump says, "Bergdorf Goodman? It's all made up!"]

RK: What happened after Mr. Trump made those statements?

Carroll: There was a flurry of attacks.

RK: Have you gotten used to it?

Carroll: I will never get used to attacks like that.

RK: People congratulated you, & positive media articles- doesn't that repair your reputation Carroll: No. RK: Are you better known now?

Carroll: By people who think I'm a liar-

Habba: Objection, she's speaking about what other people think

Judge Kaplan: Overruled

RK: When did you stop your Elle column?

Carroll: The end of 2019. RK: Do you still publish a column? Carroll: Yes, on Substack. RK: Pardon my ignorance, what is Substack?

Carroll: People can pay to read. I have 21,000 - 1800 of them are paid

RW: Have your Twitter followers increased since 2019?

Carroll: Yes.

RW: Do you make any money from your followers on Twitter?

Carroll: No. RW: Can you still freelance? Carroll: The assignments are all about Donald Trump, nothing else.

RW: How much do you earn?

Carroll: About --

Habba: Objection, specify the year.

Judge Kaplan: That's a subject for cross examination. RW: How much did you use to make, versus 2023?

Carroll: $50,000 versus in 2023, 500 thousand, I mean, 500 dollars

RW: Did you post on Twitter? Carroll: Yes. Dog videos and a Christmas message wishing people care and love. RW: Did you receive replies? Scroll through them, people will get a sense ["Shut up you chattering skeleton"]

RW: Let's show this--

Habba: Objection

Judge Kaplan: Ground? Habba: It's prejudicial. Judge Kaplan: All evidence is prejudicial against the party it is offered against

RW: Who is this from? Carroll: Someone called Nebraska Cornhusker, he writes I am a trashy whore and Trump will get back at me

Habba: Objection Judge Kaplan:

 Overruled. RW: Did he post about you yesterday?

 Carroll: So I've been told. On Truth Social

Carroll: This was posted as we were in the courtroom yesterday. "I had no idea who this woman was. PURE FICTION."

Roberta Kaplan: No further questions.

VIII: Carroll on the Cross

Judge Kaplan: Cross examination?

Habba: Give me a moment, please....Ms. Carroll, you used to live in Montana? Carroll: Yes. Habba: Fair to say it was boring to you?

Carroll: Montana is never boring. Habba: You were deposed twice by me - let's look. Do you recall saying you and your first husband, the spark was gone - sorry

Habba: You said, I came to New York to interview Fran Lebowitz-

Judge Kaplan: Can I get the transcript? Roberta Kaplan: Your Honor, I don't see the difference

Habba: May I proceed?

Judge Kaplan: No. She just said something. And you haven't provided the transcript

Judge Kaplan: Ms. Habba, we're going to do it my way in this courtroom and that's how it's going to be. You tell me the line number and I read it. Then we go from there.

Habba: I was reading --

Judge Kaplan: We are going to take a recess. You will provide me with --

Judge Kaplan: Do not read it out loud. What line numbers?

Habba: Page 14, 6 through 8. Judge Kaplan: What are you doing, offering into evidence?

Habba: I'm offering it as impeachment

Judge Kaplan: Those are 2 different things

Habba: She said too different things about Montana Judge Kaplan: She said it's great and before she said, it's not boring - that's your difference?

Habba: I can ask another question. Judge Kaplan: That would be a good idea.

Habba: You were a regular at Elaine's, right?

Carroll: Yes. Habba: It's hard to get into, isn't it?

Carroll: No, not hard.

Judge Kaplan: It doesn't exist anymore. That's why it's hard to get into

Habba: Why was it hard to get seated in the front?

Carroll: Elaine choose Habba: You were a regular & saw Mario Puzo?

Carroll: I saw Woody Allen... Habba: You were in the first row? Carroll: 4th table down from the front.

Habba: You were with Esquire?

Carroll: yes

Habba: In 1979 you were making $4000 a piece? Judge Kaplan: A piece of what? Habba: Per article... Didn't you say in 1979 you made $29,000?

Carroll: That's about right. Habba: It would be bigger to be on the cover? Carroll: I'd rather be on the inside with a story

Habba: How about a cover story?

Carroll: I consider writing-- Carroll's lawyer: Can we have a sidebar? Judge Kaplan: OK. [Whispered sidebar ensues]

They've back. Habba: When you were on the cover of New York Magazine, how much was the dress you were wearing?

Carroll's lawyer: Objection!

Judge Kaplan: Sustained.

Habba: What's the most you've made annually? Carroll: $400,000

Habba: That's a lot in today's dollars, right?

Carroll's lawyer: Objection.

Judge Kaplan: You're going to have to be more specific

Habba: You agree $400,000 in 1995 is about double that today? Carroll: Maybe.

Habba: You were on TV, too, right? Through 1997? And SNL? Carroll: Yes.

Habba: Walk us through your books. Carroll: Female Difficulties. Habba: What's the whole title?

Carroll: Sorority Sisters, Rodeo Queens, Frigid Women, Smut Stars and Other Modern Girls

Habba: What's a rodeo queen?

Carroll: You have to ride and rope, out in the West. It is difficult.

Habba: What about Frigid Women?

Carroll's lawyer: Objection

Judge Kaplan: Sustained

Habba: What about Smut Stars?

Carroll: It's an old term for pornography. Habba: What did you first tell me? Carroll's lawyer: Objection. No idea what she's doing.

Judge Kaplan: My order, I said, say how you are using transcripts. Habba: She was not afraid of porn

Carroll's lawyer: Objection.

Judge Kaplan: Sustained. Habba: How did the book sell? Carroll: It sold all 10,000 copies. Habba: What was the next book? Carroll: Biography of Hunter S. Thompson

Habba: Next?

Carroll: Two advice books - a Dog in Heat is a Hot Dog

Habba: How many copies of that book did you sell?

 Carroll: It's still selling today.

 Habba: How much in 2023?

Carroll: I don't know.

Habba: And "how a smart woman can land her dream man in six weeks" - did it do well?

 Carroll: It did well, royalties still

Habba: Then Nina Garcia took over at Elle?

Carroll's lawyer: Objection. Beyond the scope.

Habba: Was your salary lowered? Carroll: Yes. All magazine advertising was down--

Habba: Was your salary changed? Carroll:
Yes. Halved in 2018. From 120,000 to 60,000

Habba; Was that a low point for your career?
Carroll: It was a lost, being halved Habba:
Did you go on TV to promote your newest
book?

Carroll: It is my duty as a writer. Habba:

Did you do that on previous books?

 Carroll: I went on the Early Show for Mr.
Right

Carroll: So I went on more TV for that book.

 Habba: Was that prime time? Carroll: No.
Habba: How many men are in What Do We
Need Men For? Carroll: Maybe 60. Habba:
How many times is the word Trump in your
book?

Carroll: Once

Habba: And how many times did you say it
on TV?

Carroll: I didn't like to say it. Usually it was the interviewer Habba: But you do mention it often, right?

Carroll: I did it here, because that's the topic. On TV, they choose the topic

Habba: Did you mention any of the other men?

Carroll: Several were done in a humorous way

Habba: What does that mean?

Carroll: I tried to get the other stories in

Habba: You went public with your allegations in June 2019, to The Cut of NY Magazine?

Carroll: Yes

Habba: The president's response was five hours after the publication of the Cut?

Carroll: NY Magazine went online. They reached out to the White House - we never planned to do it on Friday, it's not a good day to release things. But the NYT had it

Habba: Do you know if there is a communications team at the White House?

Carroll: I don't know. Habba: I represent to you that it does - Judge Kaplan: You're not going to be representing anything, or you'll be a witness.

Habba: Did you sue over the White House statement?

Carroll: No.

Habba: You're suing over the June 21, 2019 statements, right?

Carroll: Yes. Habba: But you got online responses before President Trump said anything?

Carroll: Correct. Habba: 5 hours? Carroll: Yes

Habba: Many people called you a liar before the President made his statement --

Carroll's lawyer: She's not asking a question. Habba: I wasn't finished. It says, "You're a pathetic old hag"

Judge Kaplan: It's not in evidence.

Habba: I'm trying to get it in

Judge Kaplan: No, we are not going to read out loud a document not yet in evidence. We are going to take a break right here to 3:30 and you're going to refresh your memory about how you get a document in.

 They've back. Judge Kaplan: Ms. Habba can't use documents that are not in evidence. Jury entering! Habba: Did you receive Tweets in the 5 hours before President Trump spoke? Carroll: I hadn't seen them.

Habba: Were you tagged?

Judge Kaplan: Don't get into content!

Habba: How do you suggest I proceed? Judge Kaplan: Show it to her, ask if she recognizes it.

Habba: Do you recognize it? Carroll: Yes.

Judge Kaplan: It's not marked. It should be marked. Do it appropriately. Do it overnight. They. Need. To. Be. Premarked.

Habba: Did you anticipate the public would immediately believe your allegations? Judge Kaplan: Sidebar.

[Whispered sidebar ensues]

They've back.

Habba: So you deleted the messages - then you deleted the trash?

Carroll: I periodically delete the trash. I have an old computer.

Habba: When did you stop deleting? Carroll: During the second lawsuit, the one that went on in May

Habba: You said you receive death threats daily - but you deleted then until trial? Explain what you mean. Judge Kaplan: Explain what she means by what?

Habba: When did you stop deleting death threats?

Carroll: I had not received how many there were.

Habba: Did you receive a subpoena?

Carroll: Yes.

Habba: Did you know you had a discovery obligation?

Carroll: They were just replies, slime...
Habba: What about messages in your inbox, did you delete them?

Carroll: No.

Habba: So you have the death threats?

Carroll: I deleted them. Habba: So you-
Carroll's lawyer: Asked and answered.

 Habba: This is a very important question

Carroll's lawyer: I object to the commentary too

Carroll: I may have deleted some emails too, I'm not sure Habba: Did you give them to your lawyers?

Carroll: No.

Habba: Why not? Carroll: I don't want to upset them

Habba: Do you keep the supporting emails?

Carroll: Yes. I tend to delete questions that I know I won't use. But I have an entire label for supportive messages.

Habba: Do you control your email?

Carroll: Yes. Habba: So only you deleted them? Carroll: Yes.

Habba: Ms. Carroll, are you aware it is illegal to delete evidence?

Carroll's lawyer: Objection Habba: I move for a mistrial, evidence has been deleted Judge Kaplan: Denied and the jury will disregard everything Ms. Habba just said

Habba: You stated you were in a cocoon of love, a week after President Trump's statement?

Carroll: I did. Habba: So it appears you weren't suffering much, fair to say?

Carroll: No fair. I experienced support and a flood of slime. Both. Both. Both things occurred

Habba: But some was before the President's statement? Carroll: It was from him- Habba: Based on what? Carroll: The way they were phrased. Habba: Didn't you say you went off social media? Carroll: Sometimes I take a break, I come back for breaking news

Carroll: I take a break. One can't live by Twitter alone H

abba: Now you believe these tweets are real and not fake?

Carroll's lawyer: Objection Judge Kaplan: Sustained. Habba: On June 22 Lisa Birnbach texted you - I offer DX 11

Judge Kaplan: Is this already in?

Habba: Yes.

Judge Kaplan: Then you don't have to introduce it. Habba: You said you were confused

Carroll: I did sleep until noon Habba: So it's not accurate?

Carroll's lawyer: Objection Judge Kaplan: Sustained. Habba: You said you're glad you're not living in Montana anymore? Carroll: If you say so. Habba: Don't take my word for it. Here it is

Habba: You attracted media exposure after you came forward with these allegations against President Trump? Carroll: Yes. To promote the book I answered about President Trump.

Habba: Is he the only one you discussed?

 Carroll: It's all that asked about

Habba: Could you have mentioned others from the book? Carroll: I could have. I didn't.

Habba: If you were so damaged, why didn't you stop going on TV?

Carroll: Anderson Cooper was my last. I was done. Habba: Did you have to accept the appearances? Carroll: No. Habba: Didn't you testify you don't like talking about President Trump?

Carroll's lawyer: Objection.

Kaplan: Sustained.

Habba: Let's talk about the podcasts -- The Daily, All Ears, MeidasTouch, TrumpCast-- Carroll: Yes.

Habba: Did you say Trump? Carroll's lawyer: What does she mean?

Habba: She said she didn't like saying his name. That's a lot of appearances for someone who doesn't want to say Trump

Carroll's lawyer: Objection

 Judge Kaplan: Sustained.

That's argumentative

Habba: You don't book yourself on TV Carroll: I don't. Habba: Who pays for the publicists?

Carroll's lawyer: Objection to form, Your Honor.

Judge Kaplan: Sustained.

Habba: Ms. Carroll, status is important to you? Carroll: Yes

Habba: You still want more publicity? Carroll: I'm pretty much done with it, and with books.

Habba: Are you writing a book with Mary Trump?

Carroll: She is writing the book, I'm in charge of the comments. It's Mary's money.

Habba: Whose idea was it?

Carroll: We were talking during the pandemic. Mary put it on Substack.

Habba: Has Mary Trump sued Donald Trump? Carroll's lawyer: Objection! Judge Kaplan: Sustained.

Habba: Ms. Carroll, have you ever said anything you regretted on national television?

Carroll: Yes - Carroll's lawyer: Can we have a sidebar? Judge Kaplan: Yes. [Whispered sidebar ensues]

They're back.

Habba: Have you deleted text message and not just emails? Carroll: When I see threads I delete them.

Habba: Can we have a sidebar? Judge Kaplan: No. Habba: Ms. Carroll, have you ever gotten into arguments with Twitter users? Carroll: Possibly.

 Habba: But you said you were afraid. Did you get oral threats? Carroll: People left messages. I didn't answer. Habba: You deleted them? Carroll: I didn't know you could

 Habba: You don't know what the police would do, do you? Carroll: I think those who send messages use emails they get off of TOR, the IP address is hidden

Habba: Are you afraid they're going to come to your home? Carroll: Yes. Habba: But you never call the police

Carroll's lawyer: Objection, argumentative.

Habba: You have the same phone for four years? Carroll: Yes. Habba: Who is Carol

Martin - would you call her a confidante? Carroll: Yes. Habba: You told her you felt safe? Carroll: I do, in NYC

Habba: So was lying to Carol Martin appropriate? Carroll: Yes. Her daughter was scared. So I said I had not received threats. Habba: So you lied when you said no threats - Carroll's lawyer: Objection. That wasn't the testimony

 Habba: You have a gun - do you have a license? Carroll: No. Habba: Are you aware that you have to have a license-

Judge Kaplan: Don't even start.

Habba: Do you have bullets for the gun? Carroll: Yes. Habba: You live in this state?

Carroll: Yes.

Habba: Didn't you say you would advise people not to go to H.R.? Carroll: Yes. H.R. decides cases to benefit the company.

Habba: You did a watch party with Kathy Griffin?

Carroll: Yes.

Habba: She held up the severed head of Donald Trump?

Carroll: Yes. Habba: Ms. Carroll, have you ever said you like speaking with me?

Carroll: Yes. Habba: Is that at some level because you enjoy the attention? Carroll: I wanted people to know that woman can win. I'm 80. It's not right to try to make women be quiet.

Habba: Ms. Carroll, you were not quiet in the 1980s, right?

Carroll: Right. Habba: But after 25 years you brought this suit against the sitting President?

Judge Kaplan: You're running the repeat key too often, Ms. Habba

Habba: Who is George Conway?

Carroll: He is a lawyer who does not like Donald Trump.

Habba: Has he been on TV these days? Carroll: I think so.

I wouldn't be surprised. Judge Kaplan: We'll break now.

 [As jury files out, Trump leaves too. But the lawyers are staying - there may be more]

There was no more - Judge Kaplan left without saying more

IX. Carroll Still on the Cross

On January 18, Habba's cross examination of Carroll continued, here

All rise! Judge Kaplan: Ms. Carroll, you're still under oath. [But the jury hasn't been brought in. Some laughter] Jury entering! [Good mornings exchanged] Habba: Ms. Carroll, have you spoken to your counsel about your testimony since yesterday? Carroll: No.

Ms. Habba: I was asking you about the five-hour gap- Judge Kaplan: Ms. Habba, five hours have not been established. You might be well advised to refer to "the tap" Trump's 2d lawyer Madaio: Your Honor, this is an important point. May we have a sidebar? [it begins]

They're back from sidebar. Judge Kaplan: Ladies and gentlemen of the jury, I referred to an email, it may have been a tweet. You'll see it. Habba: The White House statement was not President Trump's statement, right? Carroll: It was not.

 Habba: You are not suing about the White House statement, or the Cut -- Judge Kaplan: This is not clear. Habba: I'm trying to clear it up. Judge Kaplan: Let's clear it up - Ms. Carroll, in The Cut it said President Trump denied, you're not suing on that?

Carroll: I am not. Judge Kaplan: You are suing about what Mr. Trump said, the second time on June 22, right? Carroll: Yes. Judge Kaplan: Now it's clear as a bell. Go on, Ms. Habba.

Habba: Before the $7000 you were paid for the Cut article - Judge Kaplan: Argumentative. Habba: Did you get paid $7000? Carroll: No, it went to my publisher. Habba: Did you receive negative tweets before? Carroll: I wasn't on Twitter in the afternoon.

Habba: You looked at the tweets in the evening? Carroll: Yes, in the hotel room. Habba: And did you look at the time they were sent? Please show the exhibit. What is this? Carroll: It's a tweet. Habba: Does it tag your account? Carroll: Yes.

Habba: This tweet says, Nothing like making up fake news... And this one says, Drop this lie. Do they tag you? Carroll: Yes. Habba: And this, is this a reply to your tweet? Carroll: Yes.

Habba: This person is called Power To the Polish [like, shoes] Judge Kaplan: The person probably meant Polish [the country] Habba (laughs) And does it tag your account? Carroll: Yes.

Carroll's lawyer: We object, under your prior rulings. Habba: This was before President Trump's statement Judge Kaplan: It is stricken. Habba: Ms. Carroll, what is this? Carroll: A tweet. Yes it tags me.

Habba: It says Your book must need pumping. At 3:22 pm

Carroll: Yes, the tweet is from 3:22 pm. Habba: And that's before President Trump's statement at 5:17 pm, right? Carroll: It seems. This one is my post. Habba: And this reply - I offer it as DX 69. Carroll's lawyer: This is cumulative. We'll stipulate before 5:17

Habba: You posted, The most dangerous woman is the woman who has nothing to lose - and this reply calls you a lying sack of sh*t - that was before the President's statement was posted, right? Carroll: Right.

Habba: They would not have been able to speak to you if you were not on Twitter at that time? Carroll's lawyer: Objection Judge

Kaplan: Sustained. It is stricken. Habba: How about this one from "Rodeo Clown"?

Habba: Is Rodeo Clown replying to you?

Judge Kaplan: Do you have many more of these? Habba: I have six more. Judge Kaplan: I'll admit them if there is no objection. But you've taken enough time on this. Habba: May I be heard? Judge Kaplan: No.

Habba: This one says, You're a joke, no one would willing touch your ugly ass, this was before 5:17 pm? Judge Kaplan: Everyone knows the time. What are the numbers? Habba: DX 72, 73, 74, 75 through 78.

Carroll's lawyer: Can we have copies? I can't read fast enough Habba: I can't ask about them? With all due respect-

Judge Kaplan: With. All. Due. Respect - when I rule, you go on. Habba: So do you- Carroll's lawyer: Objection. Judge Kaplan: Sustained. Stricken. Habba: On what basis? Judge Kaplan: Move on.

Habba: Wouldn't you agree that negative tweets are not necessarily tied to the President's statement? Carroll: They follow Donald Trump. They want to emulate him. Habba: I showed you early tweets- Carroll's lawyer: Objection

Habba: Why do you believe that? How can they emulate if they were before? Carroll: They are standing up for the man they admire. Judge Kaplan: Ms. Habba, move on Habba: Did you authorize the excerpt? Carroll: I agreed with the final edit and that it should go live

Habba: What is you Substack called? Carroll: Ask E. Jean. Habba: You make $70,000 on that? Carroll: Now it's $100,000. Habba: And there's royalties? Carroll: Yes. Habba: I hate to ask, but how old are you? Carroll: I'm 80. Habba: You make more now? Carroll: Yes

Habba: Your Substack was popular as soon as you started it in 2021? Carroll: It's a lot of work. Habba: You make a lot--

Judge Kaplan: Ms. Habba, this is Evidence 101. Ms. Carroll, when there is an objection you should sit quietly until I rule.

Judge Kaplan: Ms. Carroll what was your gross income in 2023? Carroll: $70,000. But now more, I write more --

Habba: How many subscribers? Judge Kaplan: That was definitely asked yesterday. Habba: Number of subscribers? Judge Kaplan: 1800. More on.

Habba: Do you have social security? Carroll: Yes. Habba: Do you have a pension? Carroll: No. But I do have stocks. Habba: How much? Carroll's lawyer: Objection, Your Honor. Judge Kaplan: Sustained.

Habba: Do you consider yourself a financially successful person? Carroll's lawyer: Objection! Judge Kaplan: Sustained Habba: Did you publish a text asking if a person would have sex with Donald Trump for $17,000- Carroll's lawyer: Objection Judge Kaplan: Sustained

Habba: You testified you were upset because certain tweets made you appear promiscuous, correct? Carroll: Correct.

Habba: Did you post sexually explicit tweets? Carroll's lawyer: Objection

Judge Kaplan: Sustained.

[Note for X subscribers on SDNY conflicts / disclosure here

* * *

By day's end the big question was whether Trump will come and testify Tuesday. Boris, speaking on mic while Habba headed off, said he wouldn't speak to Trump's schedule. Nor would he comment on Judge Kaplan's rulings on objections. Inner City Press will stay on the case(s)

X. Trump Not in the Courtroom

Now that Trump wasn't in the courtroom, some air went out of the balloon. Still on

Worth Street photographers waited in the freezing cold, for the entrances and hours later, the exits.

E. Jean Carroll had a security man, smaller than G. Maxwell's and SBF's, but crisp and to the point. Do not obstruct us, he'd say, as photographers and journalists holding their phones in the air were pushed back into a metal barricade. They call it news.

Up in the courtroom, the cross of Carroll sputtered to its end.

Habba: You posted, The most dangerous woman is the woman who has nothing to lose - and this reply calls you a lying sack of sh*t - that was before the President's statement was posted, right?

Carroll: Right.

Habba: They would not have been able to speak to you if you were not on Twitter at that time?

Carroll's lawyer: Objection

Judge Kaplan: Sustained. It is stricken.
Habba: How about this one from "Rodeo Clown"?

Habba: Is Rodeo Clown replying to you?

Judge Kaplan: Do you have many more of these?

...Habba: I can't ask about them? With all due respect-

Judge Kaplan: With. All. Due. Respect - when I rule, you go on.

Habba: So do you-

Carroll's lawyer: Objection.

Judge Kaplan: Sustained. Stricken.

Habba: On what basis? Judge Kaplan: Move on.

Habba: Wouldn't you agree that negative tweets are not necessarily tied to the President's statement?

Carroll: They follow Donald Trump. They want to emulate him.

Habba: Why do you believe that? How can they emulate if they were before?

Carroll: They are standing up for the man they admire.

Judge Kaplan: Ms. Habba, move on

Yes, Move On. And so it went. Online legal experts, longstanding and just-for-today, trashed Habba's performance. Kurt Wheelock idly wondered, could Habba sue for these comments? But who had sparked them? Whom did they serve?

* * *

Kurt Wheelock too had his reputation issues, however different. When he had been in the UN, haters - mostly from big media - has impersonated his Twitter account, and added insults to a Wikipedia page about him. Since he'd been thrown out, with their assistance but for larger forces - so Kurt said - the edits had slowed. But recently a single Wiki-nerd immersed in the world of Assange had merged Kurt's website name into his own, and added anonymous quotes against him from inside the UN, and little to nothing about his court reporting, here. Really? Kurt didn't sue, nor did he edit. He live-tweeted trials now, and got pushed back into metal barricades while filming. It was a free country. At least for now.

XI. Monday, Monday

On January 22, Habba spoke of COVID exposure and the NH primary. Carroll's lawyer said if Juror 3 is cleared on Tuesday, the trial should end that day -- presumably without Trump.

Note: Judge Kaplan told Carroll's lawyer, who wants to end the trial tomorrow during NH primary, without Trump in court, "you might get what you want." Interpretation: if Juror 3 is OK, evidence might end tomorrow, without Trump present - "everybody wins"

Jury entering! Judge Kaplan: Juror 3 reported that he was ill. Rather than risk him coming together and having contact with you, we sent him home. He will COVID test today and report - we will not take testimony today. 1 or 2 of the lawyers are negative after test

Judge Kaplan: Andy will tell you how to report if you have symptoms, and a number to call to find out if we are going to proceed tomorrow or not. This Court continued right through COVID, so I'm sure we'll get through this. Thank you, your transportation is coming

 Jury leaves.

 Judge Kaplan: Defense made a motion for mistrial, again. That motion is going to be denied in all respects.

Habba: The NH primary is tomorrow. My client would have to testify tomorrow. Carroll's lawyer: We want to finish tomorrow.

Judge Kaplan: Circumstances may result in you getting what you want. Or perhaps not.

Trump's 2d lawyer Madaio: We'd like to make a Daubert motion about Professor Humphreys testimony

Judge Kaplan: The time to do so was before she testified. Judge Kaplan: I'm not saying I'll view it as timely, but you could file a written motion

* * *

XII. Tough Young Teens (New Hampshire)

They were tough young teens
In ski hats saying Trump
They said Fuck the Bullshit
Make America Great again again again

Their cohort in New York
Marched against the IDF
Called Eric Adams racist
Against Palestinians

Who would run the country?
The New Yorkers bound for Wall Street

XIII. COVID in the Courts

LITERARY SDNY, Jan 22 – It was the day Trump was supposed to testify - and there on Pearl Street was the motorcade, all parked in the wrong direction, ready for the escape.

Up on the 26th floor, however, the courtroom stayed empty. In the hall US Marshals manned the metal detectors and court staffers ran in and out.   Kurt Wheelock stood by the elevator, being friendly, not pushing too hard for the inside scoop.

"He's going in," he was told - and Trump walked behind a phalanx of lawyers, from the witness room through the hall and into the courtroom. It was one, or so it seemed.

But it soon emerged that COVID would pause this trial, as it had so many others.

Juror 3 had not come in, skipping out from the pick-up point. He would have to be tested for the virus.

And Alina Habba said she had been exposed, via her parents. That she still didn't wear a mask spread like wildfire on Threads.

Trump supporters on the other hand, focused on something that Carroll's lawyer Robbie Kaplan said: that she'd like the trial to resume tomorrow, the day of the New Hampshire primary, and to end that day. You might get what you want, Judge Kaplan replied. And you might not. Kurt Wheelock wrote it up.

 By late afternoon, as Kurt covered other cases, word came that Tuesday too was canceled, and the big day would be Wednesday. Or would it be?

* * *

Why had Judge Kaplan canceled Tuesday? Was it to not preclude the defendant's testimony on the day of the primary? Or to allow the showdown that had been loomed,

Trump on the stand maybe disobeyed evidentiary rulings, the word "in contempt" in the air? Words were in the air. Would all this hoopla, now like a boxing match in Las Vegas, actually bear fruit?

What would be in it, really, for Trump to testify? By Wednesday he could probably have won the New Hampshire primary - 18 points were projected, which if it fell to 9 would be described as a Nikki Pyrrhic victory. Why take the chance? But if it were less than nine....

A reader wrote in:

Kurt Wheelock is an interesting fellow...a man of mystery...sort of like Mr. Walker* (*for the ghost who walks)

Reply

Yes, Kurt Wheelock has been around since the subprime lending crisis (book: Predatory Bender) and of course since, with the UN (Belt and Roadkill)

But what would Kurt do now?

XIV. On the Trail, New Hampshire: George Santos Sighting

LITERARY SDNY, Jan 24 – Primary Tuesday and then Wednesday, there was no Trump, not at the SDNY courthouse. [In preparation for Thursday, sources spoke to Kurt Wheelock, below and here.]

But Tuesday evening after Nikki Haley spoke, vowing to fight back to South Carolina and beyond, the Trump event had surprisingly guests.

Some focused on Alina Habba, there to the side of the podium with a wall of flags behind her. But there too was George Santos, in another room, promoting himself. But wasn't he on pre-trial release?

Hadn't he gotten it extended, in the docket, from New York to include DC before he was thrown out of Congress?

 Quickly some tried to smooth it over, saying he'd given notice of this trial. But that's not how it was supposed to work, at least not in SDNY. In the Handler case, for example, there was a letter seeking approval for a one-day trip to Ohio. The District Judge had to approve it, then add to work out the details with Pre-Trial. Details, details.

 In the Carroll case court was skipped on Wednesday too, resuming they now said on Thursday.

   Kurt Wheelock was told, They're going to put the jurors in different rows (due to COVID). He didn't immediately report it

XV. Trump Returns

LITERARY SDNY, Jan 25 – When it happened, it was brief. Very brief. In the morning Carol Martin testified, a hostile witness for the defense.

Only, she was not hostile. She said when she called E. Jean Carroll a drug addict, with her case as her drug, it was hyperbole. At the end E. Jean hugged Carol Martin.

When a phone rang in the courtroom, Judge Kaplan inquired and had the person thrown out, see below.

Judge Kaplan wanted to know exactly what Habba would ask Trump. At first Habba pushed back, then recited three questions. Judge Kaplan first approved only one, then consented to a second.

So different, it had been, with NYS Judge Engoran next door. At first he had said Trump couldn't speak at all, since he wouldn't agree to the written conditions. Then as it happened he let Trump speak, about the witch hunt and his beautiful properties, for five minutes just before lunch.

With Judge Kaplan it was after lunch. And it was not a closing argument - that would be the next day, Habba only - but rather as one of the defense's only two witnesses.

XVI. Myers and Martin Then Trump the Stand

And this was it:

OK- Carroll v. Trump 2d trial, after days' hiatus. Trump is here, Habba too.

All rise! Judge Kaplan: The jurors in seats 2 and 3 are going to be socially distanced. Carroll's lawyer Roberta Kaplan: Can we put our witness on the stand?

Judge Kaplan: Yes. Jury entering! Judge Kaplan: Good morning, I hope everyone is feeling fit today. Call your next witness.

Carroll's lawyer: We call Roberta Myers [former editor of Elle] Judge Kaplan: Record will reflect that Mr. Trump is in the courtroom. [He sits down next to Alina Habba; blue tie today]

Carroll's lawyer: Have you testified before? Myers: Yes, in the first Carroll v Trump trial.

CL: Then did you go on TV? Myers: Yes, on MSNBC   Carroll's lawyer: Who did you vote for in 2016 & 2020? Myers: Democrats.

 Carroll's lawyer: Did Elle endorse political candidates? Myers: No, that wasn't our role. We wrote profiles.

Carroll's lawyer: Were you friendly with Ms. Carroll?

Myers: Yes. But we were busy

Judge Kaplan: Cross?

Habba: I'll be brief. You don't plan to vote for Donald Trump in 2024, do you? Myers: I don't think I have to say what I plan to do Habba: Fair enough. Were you terminated by Elle?

Myers: They didn't renew my contract.

 Habba: Do you know that?

Carroll's lawyer: Objection!

Judge Kaplan: Sustained. Let's focus on the facts. Habba: You weren't at Elle when Ms. Carroll departed? Myers: I was not. Habba: So you have no knowledge from 2017 to 2019?

Myers: Nothing more than gossip. Habba: What was the gossip?

Carroll's lawyer: Objection!

Judge Kaplan: Sustained.

Habba: What kind of writer was Ms. Carroll? Myers: Journalistic. Habba: What does that mean?

Myers: Accurate. Habba: Ms. Carroll gave relationship advice, right? Myers: And she wrote about the culture.

Habba: How would she respond to questions?

Myers: She would call a psychiatrist, or an MD, an expert

Habba: So that's being a fact checking journalist?

Carroll's lawyer: Objection.

Judge Kaplan: Sustained. Habba: So what--
Judge Kaplan: I have ruled. Move on. Habba:
No more questions. Judge Kaplan: The
witness is excused.

Judge Kaplan: Any more plaintiff's
witnesses? Carroll's lawyer:

No. Just a few exhibits. Let's play the video
of exhibit 164. Habba: No objection. [Video
of Trump: "This is a rigged deal, I had no
idea who she was, nor could I care less."]

 Judge Kaplan: When was that? Habba: We
met and conferred and objected. Judge
Kaplan: This just came in without objection.
Habba: Yes, but --

Judge Kaplan: Have a seat.   Carroll's lawyer:
Next exhibit. Trump's lawyer Madaio: We
objected to this. If we can have a sidebar...
[Whispered sidebar ensues]
[They're back from sidebar & play video]

Video of Trump's April 2023 deposition
against blue background, says My most

valuable assets is the brand... I became President because of the brand. I think it's the hottest brand in the world. I did an NFT and it sold out

 Jury seeing video of Trump: And the cards, their value is up, I'm happy, Trump people. I did it. It sold out immediately. Some of the cards are selling for $20,000. One, I think, for $82,100, I heard numbers like that. Somebody hit the jackpot

 Jury seeing video of Trump saying, I believe the brand is worth more than the buildings. It's like Coke.

In video, NY AG lawyer: What's the price of Mar-a-Lago? Trump: $1.5 billion. NY AG lawyer: Here's your letter to Deutsche Bank [Trump on video stares at it]

Jury seeing video: NY AG: You showed it to Deutsche Bank commercial real estate? Trump: No, another division of the same bank. They're very separate.

Carroll's lawyer: We offer PX 167 and 167-T. Please play it [Jury sees video of another Trump deposition Q: When did you move into Trump Tower: Trump: A year after it was built.

Q: When were you married to your first wife Ivanka? Trump: 1978 to the early 90s. Jury sees deposition:

Q: When you were President, did you ever speak directly to reporters? Trump: Yes. Too many to name. Q: Did you read The Cut excerpt? Trump: I don't believe I did.

Q: And What Do We Need Men For - have you read it?

Trump: Never seen it. Jury sees deposition: Q: Did you say this, There is zero evidence, it's fake news - no sales attendants around?? All should condemn false accusation. If info if Democrats are working with Ms. Carroll, let us know. Did you say this? Trump: Yes. I stand behind it

Jury sees deposition: Q: And did you say, I'll say it with great respect, she's not my type. Trump: Yes.

Q: And you said you never met her? Trump: Yes. Later they showed me a photo from a receiving line at a charity. I shake a lot hands. Her husband, John Johnson

Jury sees deposition Q: Who is this in the photo?

Trump: It's Marla.

Q: You're saying that's Marla? It's E. Jean Carroll.

Trump: It's John Johnson... It's very blurry.

Jury sees deposition:

Q: What did you mean, She's not my type - physically? Trump: Yes. And now that I know more, not my type in any way. Q: I take it the three women you married are your type? Trump: Yes. Jury sees deposition:

Q: What is Truth Social?

Trump: It's a platform opened by me, an alternative to Twitter.

Q: You issued a statement on Truth Social?

Trump: Yes. She's sick. She made it up, contradicted by what she said on CNN

Jury sees deposition: Trump: I'll be suing her when this case is over. And I'll be suing you too. Q: Are you done? Did you write this all yourself?

 Trump: Yes. Q: You wrote, I have no idea who she is Trump: I think she's a wack job. Jury sees deposition: Q: You said the word hoax 250 times in 2020?

Trump: Probably. There are a lot of hoaxes played on me. Russia Russia Russia. Ukraine. Mueller. Lying to the FISA court - hoax. Lying to Congress - hoax by the scum we have in this country

Jury sees deposition: Trump: She's a liar and she's sick. Q: In addition to Mueller, Russia Russia Russia - did you also call mail-in ballots a hoax?

Trump: Yes. They are very dishonest. Q: But you vote by mail.

Trump: Yes. But after it in, I don't know what next

Carroll's lawyer: Your Honor, I believe we're done with our evidence - but give us the break first.

Judge Kaplan: OK, ten minutes. Jury leaves.

Carroll's lawyer: They intend to call Mr. Trump, then Ms. Martin. Judge Kaplan: Aren't there motions, after they close? Habba: Yes.

Judge Kaplan: OK. All rise!

They're back. Judge Kaplan: Is the plaintiff going to rest? Carroll's lawyer Roberta Kaplan: Yes. Judge Kaplan: Is there a motion?

Habba: Yes, under Rule 50 a-- Judge Kaplan: Rule 58 doesn't have anything to do with this.

Habba: I said 50-A, your Honor. This backlash occurred before President Trump even had an opportunity to speak. A jury can't find that. The Cut caused the harm. As 2d Circuit recognized in Samuels v. Air Transport, we are entitled to judgment as a matter of law

   Judge Kaplan: You're saying there're no causation? Habba: Yes, but I'd like to finish and make a record.

Judge Kaplan: You've made a record. But if you're going to be brief...

Habba: She has made lewd posts about p*nises and people found those tweets & responded

Habba: She intentionally deleted evidence --

Judge Kaplan: When did that deletion occur? Habba: The day The Cut came out.

Judge Kaplan: Wasn't there no anticipation of litigation until she spoke with George Conway? Habba: She continued to delete

Judge Kaplan: Is there any subpoena in the record?

Habba: It's discovery rules. We can point to her testimony --

Judge Kaplan: You've already pointed to that. But where is there a subpoena in the record? Habba: We can submit it Judge Kaplan: Not later

Judge Kaplan: These are emails that included death threats? Habba: She says so.

Judge Kaplan: You're saying she should be punished because she deleted tweets that would be helpful to her - Habba: That's not what I'm saying

Judge Kaplan: You're repeating yourself. Habba: Clearly I'm not being heard...

Their expert wasn't even aware that President Trump's statement was five hours after The Cut came out. She said, "I am not aware." She did not consider the timing

Habba: She cannot establish causation. This should not go to the jury.

Carroll's lawyer Roberta Kaplan: I'm going to be brief. There is ample evidence of causation. Mr. Trump did speak before the tweet. There was a denial in The Cut

Carroll's lawyer: The tweets overlap with what Mr. Trump said on June 21 and June 22

Judge Kaplan: There could be multiple causation. Carroll's lawyer: The response here was foreseeable based on what Mr. Trump himself said, "People should pay dearly"

Judge Kaplan: The motion is denied. Who is your first witness?

Habba: Carol Martin. But they have opened the door for me to ask my client what he meant in the deposition. Judge Kaplan: I'll hear from the plaintiff Carroll's lawyer: Your Honor ruled what he can say

Carroll's lawyer: Your Honor has ruled Mr. Trump cannot contradict the prior jury's finding. And we think it's appropriate for Ms. Habba to proffer what her client can testify.

Judge Kaplan: I'm planning on dealing with this. What about Carol Martin?

Carroll's lawyer: They want to put in new exhibits. DX 100, a text, 101, 23 and 97. We object.

Judge Kaplan: Who's going to address this for Mr. Trump?

Madaio: I will. 101 is already in evidence. The other is a text - Judge Kaplan: I'm only ask for a number

Judge Kaplan: You have had these documents a long time, true? Madaio: We intend to use it to impeach - Judge Kaplan: To impeach your own witness? Madaio: She's an adverse party

Habba: They have opened the door on the Reid Hoffman issue - they asked about George Soros and the DNC - the door is open --

Judge Kaplan: The door is closed. Let's bring in the jury.   Jury entering!

Deputy Andy: What is your name? A: Francis Carol Martin. Habba: How long have you known Ms. Carroll?

Martin: 30 years. Habba: You have counsel? Martin: I do. Habba: Did we try to interview you? Martin: You did. Habba: I'd like her declared a hostile witness. Did you last meet with plaintiff's counsel in the last month?

Martin: Twice. Habba: And did you speak with us? Martin: No. Habba: You're here under subpoena? Martin: Yes. Habba: You went to Ms. Kaplan's firm? A: Yes

Habba: Did they show you documents?

Martin: No, I'd testified twice before. Habba: Both times for Ms. Carroll? Martin: Yes. Habba: Do you use Twitter or social media?

Martin: No. I prefer to live a private life Habba: Otherwise it'd be public? Martin: It seems so

 Habba: You reviewed Ms. Carroll's book? Martin: A portion. Habba: You reviewed the Cut? Martin: Cut meaning what?

Habba: New York Magazine. Martin: Yes. Habba: Did you read the whole book? Martin: Over time, I did. Habba: When did you finish? Martin: Hard to say

Habba: Were you concerned for safety? Martin: On some levels. And for my daughter. Habba: Did you tell Ms. Carroll? Martin: Yes. Habba: How? Judge Kaplan: Is this a hypothetical question? Habba: Text, or in person - that was my question Judge Kaplan: No it wasn't

Habba: Did you put anything in an email about your safety? Martin: Yes. Habba: Did you feel better? Martin: It ebbed and flowed. The climate in the country was changing rapidly. Habba: After The Cut, were you concerned for your safety? Martin: My daughter was

Habba: Ms. Carroll told you she has zero security concerns? Martin: She did. I don't know if she said Zero. Habba: What is this? Martin: Texts from Ms. Carroll. Habba: DX 101 to impeach.

Carroll's lawyer: Objection. There's nothing to impeach.

 Habba: Your Honor, I have a right to ask her what it says. Judge Kaplan: It's in evidence.

Habba: Ms. Carroll invited you to social event about her case, yes?

Martin: Yes. Habba: Which events? Martin: I don't know. Habba: Was I arguing at them? Martin: You? No

Martin: After the NYT podcast there was interest.. There was a Harvey Weinstein sidebar... Not just E. Jean, but others as well.

Habba: Did you think Ms. Carroll was enjoying the attention? Martin: At points. Habba: Ms. Martin, what does narcissism mean to you

Martin: Seeing things through yourself- Habba: You know you're under oath? You said, Ms. Carroll's narcissism has run amuck? Martin: I texted that to a friend. Habba: I understand it's hard to see this about a friend Judge Kaplan: No speeches, Ms. Habba

Habba: Ms. Martin, you've said Ms. Carroll is a drug addict and the drug is herself, right? Martin: I don't remember. Habba: Do you see this document? Martin: It was written to my daughter. Judge Kaplan: Some to the sidebar and bring a copy of this in writing, please [Whispered sidebar ensues]

They've back Habba: Did you understand Ms. Carroll was hoping to lose this so she could go to the Supreme Court? Carroll's lawyer: Objection! Judge Kaplan: Sustained. Habba: We've going through this ad nauseum. Can you look at Judge Kaplan: Ask a proper question

 Habba: So she could sell more books? Martin: She wanted to sell her book. Habba: Do you believe that publicity has become part of her lifestyle? Martin: It's an extension of the lifestyle she already had

Habba: Yes or no.

Martin: I'm hard pressed to say

Habba: Did she celebrate this case? Martin: It was organized by journalists. Habba: What journalists?

Martin: There were more than one. Habba: Who do they write for? Martin: From the NY Times? Martin: I don't know.

Habba: Any from Fox News?

Martin: Not that I know

Habba: How many parties about these lawsuits against Mr. Trump? Martin: Six I went to. Habba: Which one with journalists? Martin: I don't remember. Habba: Did these journalists write articles about her case?

Carroll's lawyer: Objection!

Judge Kaplan: Sustained

Habba: Were you frustrated by these parties about the lawsuit?

Martin: Somewhat. We are different. Habba: What about the dinner - where there lawyers there? Martin: Robbie was there.

Habba: And George Conway? Martin: No. Habba: You stated that Ms. Carroll was acting a little scary, didn't you? Martin: Bad choice of words. Habba: That's a yes? Martin: Yes. Habba: You said she was loving the adulation?

 Martin: Yes. Habba: Did you share with others private messages Ms. Carroll sent you? Like DX 100? I offer it Carroll's lawyer: I object.

Habba: It's for impeachment.

Judge Kaplan: Let me have a legible copy.

Judge Kaplan: Objection sustained. Habba: But you have shared Ms. Carroll's private messages? Martin: I really don't remember. Habba: Do you see that you sent this to--

Judge Kaplan: Sustained. You are reading a document not in evidence

Habba: Do you believe Ms. Carroll is enjoying this fame? Martin: I think she is adapting. Enjoying is a multi-faceted word.

Habba: No further questions. Judge Kaplan: Cross? Carroll's lawyer: You know Ms. Carroll has been harmed because you're friends?

 Madaio: Objection!

Judge Kaplan: She's Ms. Habba's witness.

Habba: Objection!

Judge Kaplan: Overruled. Carroll's lawyer: Were you named in the book? Martin: It was dedicated to me and Ms. Birnbach. In the book I was identified as a news reporter. Carroll's lawyer: And did you-- Habba: Objection! We discussed all of this before. Happy to talk sidebar

They're back. Carroll's lawyer: Ms. Martin, you were concerned about your safety? Martin: Once I spoke with a NYT podcast.

Q: Were you concerned because you'd been involved in Ms. Carroll's lawsuit against Donald Trump?

Habba: Objection! Judge Kaplan: Overruled

Martin: US climate felt dangerous to me.
Carroll's lawyer: What did you mean about
lifestyle? Martin: That the lawsuit had
become a large part of her life

Carroll's lawyer: You were concerned it
wouldn't work out for her?

Habba: Objection!

Judge Kaplan: Overruled

Carroll's lawyer: You discussed the passage
of the NY law allowing her to sue Donald
Trump for sexual assault?

Habba: Objection! I never asked about that.

Judge Kaplan: But you alluded to it.
Overruled. Carroll's lawyer: You didn't want
her to file a 2d lawsuit? Martin: He was
saying he hadn't lost the 2020 election -

Habba: Objection Judge

Kaplan: Overruled. Carroll's lawyer: Why
were you concerned? Martin: That the
defamation would just continue and escalate.

Carroll's lawyer: What did you mean, Drug addict? Martin: No idea. I use words too loosely sometimes. Carroll's lawyer: Since Ms. Carroll had been a journalist her whole life, it is not surprising there were journalists at her parties?

Martin: Right

Carroll's lawyer: Do you think Ms. Carroll is a narcissist? Martin: I have no idea. Carroll's lawyer: Do you distrust her motives?

Martin: No. Carroll's lawyer: What was her job when you get her? Martin: A columnist. Then in 1994 we did TV shows for America Talks

Carroll's lawyer: Do you think Ms. Carroll wants to be known as the woman who lied about the president sexually assaulting her?

Habba: Objection!

Judge Kaplan: Overruled. Martin: No. Carrol's lawyer: No further questions.

Judge Kaplan: We'll take our break. Lawyers be back at ten of two. Jurors, you'll have a bit longer. I have some business to do with them.

[Note: in SBF trial, Judge Kaplan had SBF do a mock testimony without the jury]

Jury leaves.

XVII: Trump on the Stand

They're back. Judge Kaplan: Ms. Habba, do you have any other witnesses? Habba: Yes, President Trump. Judge Kaplan: I have a few things to say

Judge Kaplan: There was a trial last year about the truth or falsity of Ms. Carroll claims. Mr. Trump was listed as a witness but did not testify. The jury found for Ms. Carroll. There are no do-overs, it's called issue preclusion or collateral estoppel.

Judge Kaplan: The jury found that Mr. Trump inserted his fingers into her v*gina. And that Ms. Carroll did not make up her claim. And that Mr. Trump's June 11 and June 22 statements were defamatory. Now Mr. Trump may not make any argument against this

Judge Kaplan: Ms. Carroll adhered to the Court's rulings. Ms. Kaplan on behalf of Ms. Carroll questioned if Mr. Trump could offer any admissible testimony. Ms. Habba, you said he could testify about the reporters' questions, and if he was acting with ill will

Judge Kaplan: A judge must seek to exclude inadmissible evidence. Concerns exist here, as including in Ms. Kaplan's letter. I want to confirm a few things. Ms. Habba, what would he testify to?

Habba: I have only three questions for my client.

Judge Kaplan: We're going to do it my way.

Habba: He's going to stand by his deposition. That he had to respond to accusation and deny them. Judge Kaplan: That's 100%?

Habba: I'm not testifying for my client

Judge Kaplan: Let me hear from the other side.

Roberta Kaplan: Just now Mr. Trump said under his breath he's going to say he never did it.

Judge Kaplan: He will not testify about questions asked of him by reporters?

Habba: No. If I may you Honor--

Judge Kaplan: No

Judge Kaplan: What are your questions? Habba: That he stands behind his deposition. I'll ask about his state of mind, he'll say he was defending himself --

Judge Kaplan: And that's it? Habba: Yes. And that he never intended to hurt Ms. Carroll. Roberta Kaplan: He had an opportunity to participate in a trial--

Judge Kaplan: And he lost. I will so instruct the jury. More than once. Trump says, "I wasn't at the trial, I never met this woman

Judge Kaplan: Mr. Trump, keep your voice down. Judge Kaplan: Will your client abide?

Habba: Absent having a glass ball

[Trump is speaking]

Judge Kaplan: Mr. Trump, that is not allowed... I will permit him to get on the stand. You ask if he stands by it. That's it.

Habba: Only one question?

Judge Kaplan: You can ask the 2d question. Habba: "Why did you make the statements"-

Judge Kaplan: No. Habba: I have a right to ask about intent.

Judge Kaplan: I will decide what he has a right to do here. That's my job, not yours

Habba: I can ask it that way-- Judge Kaplan: It will not be an open-ended question. If you ask it, there is likely to be an objection and I am likely to sustain it. Habba: That's it. Judge Kaplan: OK.

Habba: What about 2d question? Judge Kaplan: It keeps changing

Habba: As long as we have the deposition in, I think I'll be fine.

Judge Kaplan: Well, I hope you will.

 [Jury entering!]

 Judge Kaplan: I hope lunch was better than the cafeteria usually is. Ms. Habba you may call your witness.

Habba: Defense calls President Donald Trump...

Trump: Donald John Trump. Habba: You viewed your deposition?

Trump: I stand by it 100%, yes.

Trump: She said something I considered a false accusation --

Roberta Kaplan: Objection!

Judge Kaplan: Sustained.

Habba: I have no further questions.

Judge Kaplan: Cross examination.

Roberta Kaplan: There was a trial here, correct?

Trump: Yes

Roberta Kaplan:

Mr. Trump, is this the 1st trial between you and Ms. Carroll you've attended?

Trump: Yes.

Roberta Kaplan: No further questions.

 Habba: Did you have counsel at the previous trial & follow their advice?

Trump: Yes.

Roberta Kaplan: Objection

Sustained

Habba: No further questions.

Judge Kaplan: Jurors, you may go until tomorrow morning, closing arguments. [Jury leaves]

Judge Kaplan: Counsel can pick up the draft jury charge at 2:30, we have to run the copier. Charge conference...

XVIII. Charge Conference

Trump's lawyer: We seek to limit this instruction Judge Kaplan: But you previously argued that under New York law Mr. Trump could have been found to have committed sexual assault if he touched her breast --

Trump's lawyer: That was previous counsel

Judge Kaplan: That's Mr. Trump's counsel, his argument. It was found in the previous case that there was digital penetration. Under penal law [there's some laughter] Judge Kaplan: How do you proposed we describe it? Digital penetration? Trump's lawyer Madaio: There's no need for the jury to hear any of this.

Judge Kaplan: Mr. Madaio, I'm giving you one more chance.

Trump's lawyer Madaio: What the jury found was sexual abuse- Judge Kaplan: You're just repeating yourself.

Madaio: You know our objections. Judge Kaplan: I do. Objection overruled.

Judge Kaplan: The jury is clearly entitled to award punitive damage to deter the defendant from continuing to defame the plaintiff... Or anyone else for that matter. Judge Kaplan: So I think we're done, counsel. I appreciate the cooperation on both sides. [Judge Kaplan leaves]

* * *

During the trial day, a phone went off in Judge Kaplan's courtroom. "Whose phone is that?" he said. "Have that man removed." It was Steven Cheung.

In the charge conference after Trump had done, Judge Kaplan shut down most of Madaio's objections. So it wasn't just Habba - it was the defense team as a whole. The jurors were just being asked how much Trump should pay, for the two statements but also to deter the type of statements they heard from later. But would any of those selected say no, it was too much? Kurt Wheelock went back over what he had tweeted during voir dire - and what he had written in his reporter's notebook. Watch this platform.

XIX. The Final Day

The final day began with closing arguments. Trump came in late and Judge Kaplan noted it. During Robert Kaplan's closing, Trump stood up and walked out - and again Judge Kaplan noted it. Trump returned for his lawyer Habba's closing - then was locked in the courtroom for Judge Kaplan's instructions. "He put his fingers in her vagina."

The jury began deliberating, and there were no notes. It was almost 4:30 when word circulated that a verdict had been reached. Trump had left a half an hour before. Perhaps it was for that best. When it came, it was punitive: $65 million in punitive damages, to be exact. Total of $83.3 million.

Outside Carroll went to her waiting four by four without commenting, only smiling. Kurt Wheelock was there, filming then did a stand-up. When Habba came out someone shouted, Will you stop representing Trump?

No, she said - and took to the microphone. It was a witch hunt and President Trump wouldn't give in. This was why people liked President Trump, she said. Some people.

XX. Closing Argument of Carroll

OK- Carroll v. Trump 2d trial closing arguments - and jury deliberations. Trump is here in SDNY - but not in the courtroom yet.

Judge Kaplan: I notice the defense is not yet in the courtroom... [Then]

Judge Kaplan: Now Mr. Madaio is in the courtroom. [Habba enters.]

Judge Kaplan: Ms. Habba, it is now twenty minutes to ten. Habba: I'm sorry, I can't hear you. Judge Kaplan: Does your client intend on being present?

Habba: He's here.

Judge Kaplan: He's not in the courtroom. Habba: I can grab him... [Trump enters]

Judge Kaplan: So let me say, during the arguments and instructions, no one else is to speak...

Carroll's lawyer: We have an issue with some of the tweets, they were not entered into evidence.

Madaio: These are tweets during the five-hour gap. They are objecting.

Judge Kaplan: You did not succeed in entering them. Show me the slide

Judge Kaplan: You are not showing the slide.

Habba: Your Honor, Ms. Kaplan stipulated -

Judge Kaplan: Sit down. You are on the verge of spending some time in the lock up.

(Habba appears to laugh)

Judge Kaplan: Bring in the jury

Roberta Kaplan: Donald Trump's testimony yesterday was brief because he doesn't get a do-over Trump's lawyer

Madaio: Objection!

Judge Kaplan: Overruled.

Roberta Kaplan: This is about how to compensate Ms. Carroll for the two statements- & punishing Donald Trump

Roberta Kaplan: This trial is about getting him to stop once and for all. It's also about whether the rules apply to all, including to Donald Trump. Think of his attitude to this proceeding - he says, She was asking for it

Roberta Kaplan: He claims he had no choice but to break the law and defame her. She was a beloved advice columnist. Then a wave on social media, echoing what Donald Trump says. Let's consider: in 2019 he said "pay dearly" and "dangerous territory." Roberta Kaplan: Donald Trump has tried to normalize this conduct. Normally, when people lose in court, they change their behavior.

[Trump leaves]

Judge Kaplan: The record will reflect that Mr. Trump just rose and left the courtroom

Roberta Kaplan: Mr. Carroll's old friend Carol Martin said she just wanted her day in court. Now she has it. Judge Kaplan: We're going to change gears. The defense is to remain seated. That includes you, Mr. Epshteyn, not that you're part of the defense

Roberta Kaplan: Ms. Carroll's success as an advice columnist obviously relied on her audience's trust. She built it over decades. She had one truth too painful to share - in the Spring of 1996 Donald Trump sexually assaulted her. She tried to suppress it

Roberta Kaplan: Her 274-page book contained nine pages about Donald Trump. New York Magazine published that. Donald Trump then told lie after lie after lie, to destroy her. Put up Slide 4 [It is entitled, Defamatory Statement: disgrace... never met this person]

 Roberta Kaplan: Donald Trump was lying and trying to destroy Ms. Carroll. On the White House lawn he repeated it, claiming that he didn't know her. He threatened her - People have to be careful, because they're playing with very dangerous territory

Roberta Kaplan: He said, She is not my type. This was designed to humiliate Ms. Carroll. But remember, he mistook Ms. Carroll for Marla Maples, his ex-wife, also a beauty queen. Show the video [on video: Trump: "that's John Johnson... And that's Marla...]

Roberta Kaplan: Then he claimed the photo was blurry. It is not. This was classic Donald Trump. Now, the damages. Obviously Ms. Carroll suffered harm... She now has only 1800 paying customers on Substack. Professor Humphreys gave you the estimates of harm

Roberta Kaplan: Prof Humphreys estimates between 7 and 12 million dollars to repair reputation - smaller than other programs, as she explained. Madaio: Objection. It's not in the record. Roberta Kaplan: It is. Judge Kaplan: The defense asked about other programs

Roberta Kaplan: She told you about the case of Rudi Giuliani and the Georgia elections workers - Madaio: Objection! Judge Kaplan: It's up to the jury.

Roberta Kaplan: Imagine being Ms. Kaplan in that hotel room on 10th Avenue, struck by fear and sadness - the man who attacked her was coming after her again. She wanted to close the curtain. So she hung up jump suit - she was unable to sleep

Roberta Kaplan: There were more threats waiting for her every time she answered her phone. She tweeted, the world needs love - the responses were, "you are a c*nt" and "no way Trump touched this mess," etc. Since 2019 they have never stopped

Roberta Kaplan: The dollar number to compensate her has to be very large. At least as much as $12 million for the reputational repair campaign, and probably more. And how much will it take to get Donald Trump to stop? Punitive damages are to punish the malicious

Roberta Kaplan: Consider what Donald Trump has done here. He said she made it up, she was a disgrace; he threatened her twice, he unleashed millions of others to flood her with hate. We played his deposition - he called her mentally sick, and threatened to sue

Roberta Kaplan: Watch this CNN Town Hall

[Trump: My poll numbers went up [audience cheers] I have no idea who this woman is, she is a wack job] Roberta Kaplan: Did you see that? The audience laughed. It made Ms. Carroll feel horribly

Robert Kaplan: His attacks have intensified. While Ms. Carroll was still on the stand, he held a press conference - while you were still sitting the jury box - watch this

[Video of 40 Wall Street press conference: It's a rigged deal, it's a made up fabricated story

 Roberta Kaplan: Last Thursday he said, I've said it a thousand times, I never heard of E Jean Carroll and would never touch her. Are you kidding me? A thousand times? It's up to you to make him stop. He is very wealthy. He said his brand is worth $10 billion

Roberta Kaplan: He said Mar-a-Lago is worth $1.5 billion

Madaio: Objection. These are not personal assets.

Judge Kaplan: Overruled. The jury will remember what was said.

Roberta Kaplan: You can award punitive damages. Yesterday my cross showed he didn't come to 1st trial - but he came to this one - well until just now - because he cares about money. So your decision is the only hope

Roberta Kaplan: Donald Trump can't even deny -

Madaio: Objection

Roberta Kaplan: ...he can't deny because of the first trial...

Your Honor, can I go on? Judge Kaplan: I overrule[d] Roberta Kaplan: Donald Trump had been famous for years. Why did Ms. Carroll wait?

Roberta Kaplan: The so-called gap? Give me a break. The White House, which was run by Mr. Trump, had already denied - Madaio: Objection. Judge Kaplan: Overruled.]

Roberta Kaplan: Judge Kaplan will tell you that a person who has been defamed has no duty to mitigate. Donald Trump's defense table, the first very day, made an argument that has no basis in law. They're saying she had a duty to keep her mouth shut.

Roberta Kaplan: Donald Trump claims she actually benefited. It takes a lot of gall to make an argument like that. Donald Trump's lawyer described Ms. Carroll as a fame-seeking monster-

Habba: Objection!

Judge Kaplan: The jury will recall what was said

Roberta Kaplan: I'm going to sit down in a couple of minutes, I promise. On behalf of E. Jean and our whole team, thank you for paying attention to the evidence which was ugly. How much will it take to fix her reputation? Between 7 to 12 million. We say 12.

Roberta Kaplan: Next, we say another $12 million, probably much more. On punitives, I'm not going to tell you exactly how much. You can consider his wealth. Donald Trump is worth billions of dollars, he said that under oath. This will take an unusually high award

Roberta Kaplan: When you deliberate later today, consider we have a former President of the US who has shown contempt for the rule of law and our system of justice. Stand up for E. Jean Carroll and the rule of law.

Roberta Kaplan: If not, none of us would ever be safe from bullies. There is a way: you have the opportunity, maybe even the responsibility, to put an end of this right now with your verdict - make him pay for what he has done

Roberta Kaplan: Now is the time to make him pay for it... dearly.

Judge Kaplan: Thank you, Ms. Kaplan.
We'll take a ten-minute break.

XXI. Trump's Closing

They're back. Habba: Good morning, ladies and gentlemen. Counsel tried to tell you what my arguments are. I've never seen that. We've watched plaintiff try to pin Twitter trolls on the President of the US. Here he is reacting last year [Video: This a witch hunt

Habba: I want to thank plaintiff's counsel for playing that for me. Yes, that's how he feels. Imagine a world when someone accuses you and you can't speak. She said Ms. Carroll defended herself - she said that, just now: a right to defend. What's good for thee? Habba: She's right, he has not wavered. Because it is the truth.

Roberta Kaplan: Objection!

Judge Kaplan: Sustained - that has been proved false. As I will instruct the jury.

Habba: Her bankrollers are paying -

Roberta Kaplan: Objection!

Judge Kaplan: Sustained. Ms. Habba, if you continue you may face consequences.

Habba: The White House denial in an article Ms. Carroll spread all over social media - not part of this suit

Habba: Ms. Carroll cannot. Prove. Causation. She gave her story to The Cut, she said, they knew how to break the news. She was looking to make a splash. On June 21, 2019 at 12:14 it went live - it ignited a media storm. President Trump did not know for 5 hours

Habba: Before that, a flood of tweets responded. Before President Trump even made a statement. She said there were messages of love and support, and also attacks. This five-hour gap is essential.

Habba: You are not here to pay Ms. Carroll for people who wrote mean tweets to her. No. They have to prove a direct causal connection to his two statements.

Habba: This is the beauty and danger of free speech in America. President Trump does not control the speech of others. Before and after President Trump's statement, both of these statements said Ms. Carroll did it to promote her book. Frankly, her friend said that

Habba: Ladies and gentlemen, I have received three threats this week --

Judge Kaplan: Counsel, that was inappropriate. Jury will disregard.

Habba: They have six threats, only from 2023. Why not before? She deleted them. Or perhaps they didn't exist

[Trump is at the defense table, listening]

Habba: She deleted the evidence she wants you to rely on. They are not here. She has to give them to you. They are not here. She took the stand and said she received death threats the day of the Cut, was in a "trance"

Habba: She didn't call the police - but she hung the pants. She didn't tell anyone - but she hung the pants. Focus on the details, not the noise.

Habba: There are two versions of E. Jean Carroll - the one her friend told you about, and the one who comes to court to get money from my client... Ladies and gentlemen, you heard him testify, that he didn't intend to hurt her. Habba: All he did was tell his truth.

Roberta Kaplan: Objection!

Judge Kaplan: I'll deal with it in my instruction.

Habba: My feelings would be hurt to. But it happens when you are a public figure. Just ask E. Jean - she said she was fabulous, she was carefree

Habba: She has always craved fame. She expressed it privately to Lisa Birnbach, that she was fine as fine, that she slept until noon.

She didn't think you'd see that. That's her best friend. But on the stand she claimed it wasn't true

Habba: And she hasn't suffered professionally. She didn't lose her advice column because of my client - it's because she lost her column at Elle. Before she conveniently came out with this claim Roberta Kaplan: Objection! Judge Kaplan: Sustained.   Habba: Another tweet of hers: what can be done about the p*nis? I'm mortified I have to repeat this

Habba: Here she tweets, How to dominate a man. [Pauses]

Dominate a man. She didn't take it down. She wrote, He will soon regret he even has a p*nis. Is that a threat?

 Roberta Kaplan: Objection!

Judge Kaplan: Sustained

Habba: Now she's claiming other people's tweets made her look scandalous? Numbers don't lie - these are the views and the tweets sent to Ms. Carroll - only five views, fifteen views - these are the ones they picked, to show you her damage

Habba: She's enjoying this. She is making more money today than she was in June of 2019 when she brought this up. She had hid financial rock bottom. Elle Magazine cut her salary in half, no more dinners at Elaine's, just a cottage in the wood, like Montana

Habba: She had been writing the book for years - then put in President Trump while he was in the White House. She sat in her cabin far from the glamor of New York. So she made her way - release of The Cut, she made money. She got publicists, lunch with journalists

Habba: Her best friend said Ms. Carroll love the adulation from this lawsuit, that she was acting like Santa at the Christmas parade. She said Ms. Carroll is a drug addict and the drug is herself, in a communication that she never thought you'd see

Habba: Do you think she wants her old reputation back? To go back to the cabin, with 12000 followers on Twitter? I asked her, After this are you done? She wouldn't answer. She yearned for this. She had nothing to lose and everything to gain.

Habba: They picked as their expert Ms. Humphreys. Her report was riddled with mistakes - she can't find 17 errors we found --

Roberta Kaplan: Objection!

Judge Kaplan: Sustained.

Habba: Your Honor - Judge Kaplan: Sustained! Habba: She said, Republicans were more likely to not believe Ms. Carroll than non-Republicans. Duh! Duh! Thank you Ms. Humphreys. You need an expert to make that point. People are entitled to their opinions. Who do you want you to fix it? Give her money

Habba: Their expert has never done a reputation repair campaign. She said Joe Rogan and Candace Owens could repair her reputation. What planet is she living on? Now during the trial she changed her setting on social media to private. She could have done it before

Habba: Imagine you are living your life. You have a family, a beautiful wife, and an important job to do. You're hit with an allegation. There are no facts -

Roberta Kaplan: Objection! Judge Kaplan: Sustained. Habba: She doesn't even know what I was saying

Judge Kaplan: Move onto another topic

Habba: Under the First Amendment you have a right to speak -

Roberta Kaplan: Objection!

Judge Kaplan: Sustained

Habba: You've heard the objections, you've heard me being told to sit down Robert Kaplan: Objection Judge: Move on

Habba: This is not about Ms. Carroll & Donald Trump. This is about tweeters in their mother's basement. Ms. Carroll has been made whole-

Roberta Kaplan: Objection!

Judge Kaplan: Sustained.

Habba: Ladies and gentlemen, sorry you had to spend so much time on this.

XXII. Carroll's Rebuttal

Judge Kaplan: Rebuttal?

Carroll's 2d lawyer Crowley: I'm going to follow the court's rules, unlike Mr. Trump and her lawyer. Ms. Habba said there was a five-hour gap. But there's no evidence of this gap-

Madaio: Objection!

Judge Kaplan: Overruled   Judge Kaplan: She showed you only five tweets- Habba: Objection! Judge Kaplan: Only one lawyer. Who is it?

Habba: Michael. Michael Madaio: Objection. Judge Kaplan: Overruled. Crowley: Donald Trump assaulted Ms. Carroll

Judge Kaplan: I told counsel to remain seated but they won't

Crowley: Thank you Your Honor. Donald Trump is saying, She asked for it. I have to ask: are you really still doing that? Have we not moved on? I think we have

Crowley: She didn't ask to be called ugly, or a liar. Ms. Carroll didn't ask for death threats. She gave interviews because she had to defend herself. She brought this lawsuit to try to get him to stop. You can't equate their conduct

 Crowley: When Donald Trump told those lies he was breaking the law. And he's still breaking the law to this day-

Madaio: Objection!

Judge Kaplan: Overruled.

Crowley: Donald Trump is responsible. What could be more on brand for Donald Trump than malice?

Crowley: He is breaking the law- Madaio: Objection, it's on appeal Judge Kaplan: Overruled. Crowley: You can respond to true charges by staying silent, or apologize. If he'd done that, do you think people would have come after her?

Crowley: They're suggesting Ms. Carroll has to show she'd been broken every day for five years. In their view every day she showed a brave face she was showing she suffered no harm. That makes no sense. Two things can be true at the same time. Crowley: This five-hour gap? There's no evidence.

Madaio: Objection.

Judge Kaplan: I'll rely on the jury to look at the evidence closely.

Crowley: Trump's initially denial which was issued by the White House- Madaio: Objection!

Judge Kaplan: Overruled

Crowley: The White House statement said - Madaio: Objection, it's not in evidence. Judge Kaplan: I'll see you at the sidebar [whispered sidebar ensues, mid-rebuttal They're back. Judge Kaplan: The objection is overruled. Continue, counsel

Crowley: Thank you, your Honor. The denial in The Cut, it didn't say she would pay dearly. His followers latched onto it. They keep saying it four years later

Madaio: Objection

Overruled

 Crowley: Donald Trump kept defaming Ms. Carroll - Madaio: Objection! Judge Kaplan: Overruled. Crowley: They keep coming after her. No causation? Give me a break. About Professor Humpreys. She was the only expert here

 Madaio: Objection!

Judge Kaplan: Overruled

Crowley: Professor Humphreys, the mislabeling is a distraction. Their last complaint is that she didn't consider the positive responses - this shows they don't understand what Prof Humphreys did in this case. It's about changing minds

 Crowley: The law of defamation is about protection people from harm when people lie about that. You only have to change the minds of the people who believe the lie. Ms. Habba went on about deleting some of the death threats. Ms. Habba got it wrong to mislead you

Crowley: She had no duty not to delete- Madaio: Objection Judge Kaplan: Sustained in part. I'm not going to detail which part just now. Jurors, you decide if this matters to you

Crowley: She said she deleted some of the nasty replies. She had no obligation to keep

Crowley: I think we can understand why she wouldn't want to keep these? Who among us hasn't deleted a nasty tweet or email? These are death threats from people who believed HIS lies, and expanded on HIS threats.

Crowley: You're going to hear Judge Kaplan's instructions on the law. Then you'll decide how much Donald Trump is going to pay. He wants you to blame her, that Donald Trump is the victim here.

Crowley: Her so called salacious tweets? She was reposting readers' questions. She was doing her job. They want to stop her. According to the defense, he gets to ignore a jury verdict. You saw how he behaved at trial - he walked out while Ms. Kaplan was speaking

Crowley: This is not a political rally. This is a court of law. Donald Trump is not the victim. Make him pay enough so that he will stop. Thank you.

Judge Kaplan: I will now deliver the jury charge.

Deputy Andy: Marshals, please lock the doors ...

Judge Kaplan: When you retire you will select one juror as the foreperson. The foreperson will send out any notes and will notify the officer when a verdict has been reached. Judge Kaplan: Your answer to one question will determine your answers to some following, in some places. Whatever you do, just answer the questions. I tell you from experience - you are not to add any commentary, no extraneous remarks. Answer on 1 copy

Judge Kaplan: At the bottom, put your juror number, not your name. Place the verdict in an envelope, I will ask for it. Each of you should be in agreement with verdict. Once announced it ordinarily can't be revoked.

Judge Kaplan: We can read back testimony to you, or sometimes submit it to you in writing. Only ask if you actually need it. You took an oath to rule only on the evidence. Judge Kaplan: This Court was the first in the United States. Since those first days, jurors like you have been asked to decide cases. I am sure you will be just. Counsel, any objections to my instructions?

[Sidebar] Judge Kaplan: I left one word out: "not" Judge Kaplan: The exhibits will be sent into the jury room. That normally takes a bit of time. I ask counsel to stay near the courtroom so we can respond. Your lunch is waiting for you - so 45 minutes, they are free to go -

Andy, swear the Marshall. The officer.

 Judge Kaplan: We will break at 4:30 pm if there is no verdict, unless you send a note that you would like to stay somewhere later. [No pizza like in US v. Sam Bankman-Fried final day?]

Judge Kaplan: Andy will take the exhibits. Videos on a laptop. Judge Kaplan: Anything else we have to do before we go off and have lunch? None? OK

OK - at 4:16 pm, and E. Jean Carroll's lawyers have taken their positions at plaintiff's table. So far the defense table is empty.

Now at 4:20 pm, E. Jean Carroll at plaintiff's table. Still no one at defense table.

Word is, there is a verdict. Still no one at defense table

XXIII.   Verdict

Drum roll, 5 minute warning: "Please be advised that a verdict has been reached in the above action and will be read in open court at 4:35PM"

As we wait, the first question will be: "Did Ms. Carroll prove, by a preponderance of the evidence, that 1. Ms. Carroll suffered more than nominal damages as a result of Mr. Trump's publication of the June 21 and June 22, 2019 statements?"

Judge Kaplan: I'm advised the jury has reached a verdict. We will have no outbursts in these proceedings, we will maintain decorum. Bring in the jury.

Jury entering!

Judge Kaplan: Please hand the verdict to Andy... Thank you. Clerk will read the verdict

Andy: Did Ms. Carroll prove, by a preponderance of the evidence, that 1. Ms. Carroll suffered more than nominal damages as a result of Mr. Trump's publication of the June 21 and June 22, 2019 statements? Answer Yes.

Andy (clerk): 7.3 million... 11 million... punitives: $65 million

Judge Kaplan; Members of the jury, there was years ago a respected judge of this court would made it a practice never to thank a jury. Judge Weinfeld thought it was a duty - I think juries should be thanked

Judge Kaplan: If you wish to speak after the verdict - I order you not to disclose the names of any other juror, and I advise you not to disclose your own name.

Judge Kaplan: The transportation arrangements have been made. Enjoy the weekend. [Jury leaves]

Judge Kaplan: Any other business?

Ms. Habba: I would just like to thank the court staff Judge

Kaplan: You're welcome on their behalf. Adjourned

XXIV. The End

Kurt Wheelock, still banned from the UN, was asked to comment on that day's International Court of Justice decision about Gaza. What impact would it have? And see how the UN's Antonio Guterres laundered the belated admission that his own UNRWA staff took part in the October 7 slaughter in Israel amid the ICJ news.

Kurt mused about how the two proceedings were similar, loud and widely reported but perhaps having less impact than was claimed, over Trump and Israel, sure of grievance, like Sri Lanka Sinhalese, that silent majority, dangerous...

Kurt would go from the trial to the trail.

* 9 7 9 8 8 7 7 5 8 9 4 5 2 *